D1273097

# THE DRAMATIC SYMPHONY

*and*

# THE FORMS OF ART

# Andrei Biely

## THE DRAMATIC SYMPHONY
*Translated by Roger and Angela Keys*

*and*

## THE FORMS OF ART
*Translated by John Elsworth*

GROVE PRESS, New York

English language translation of *The Dramatic Symphony*
© Roger Keys 1986.
Introduction and notes to *The Dramatic Symphony* © Roger Keys 1986.

English language translation of *The Forms of Art* © Dr. John Elsworth 1986.
Introducton and notes to *The Forms of Art* © Dr. John Elsworth 1986.

All rights reserved.

No part of this book may be reproduced, stored in a retrieval system, or
transmitted in any form, by any means, including mechanical, electronic,
photocopying, recording or otherwise, without prior written permission
of the publisher.

Published by Grove Press, Inc.
920 Broadway
New York, N.Y. 10010

English language edition first published in Great Britain in 1986 by
Polygon Books.

Library of Congress Cataloging-in-Publication Data

Bely, Andrey, 1880–1934.
    The dramatic symphony; and, The forms of art.

    Translation of: Dramaticheskaia simfoniia [and] Formy iskusstva.
    1. Bely, Andrey, 1880–1934—Translations, English. I. Bely, Andrey,
1880–1934. Formy iskusstva. English. 1987. II. Title: Dramatic symphony.
III. Title: Forms of art.
PG3453.B84 1987      891.78′309      86-45259
ISBN 0-394-55550-3

Design by Tim Robertson
Manufactured in the United States of America
First Edition 1987

10  9  8  7  6  5  4  3  2  1

# CONTENTS

INTRODUCTION                                          *page* 1

THE DRAMATIC SYMPHONY                                        17

A NOTE ON "THE FORMS OF ART"                                155

THE FORMS OF ART                                            159

# ACKNOWLEDGEMENTS

Several people have offered invaluable advice on the translation of Bely's *Dramatic Symphony*. The translators are grateful to them all, but would like to thank in particular Dr John Elsworth, the Revd. J. Dudley Johns and Mr Julius Telesin.

# IN PLACE OF A FOREWORD

The exceptional form of the present work obliges me to say a few words by way of explanation.

This work has three levels of meaning: musical, satirical and beyond these the ideal-symbolical.[1] In the first place the task of the Symphony is to express a series of moods, linked by a primary mood or harmony. Hence the necessity of dividing it into parts, of dividing the parts into fragments and the fragments into verses (musical phrases). The repetition of certain musical phrases emphasises this division.

The second level is satirical: the ridiculing of certain extremes of mysticism. The question arises of how to motivate a satirical attitude to individuals and events whose very existence is doubtful for a very large number of people. Instead of replying I can only advise people to take a closer look at the reality surrounding them.

Finally, beyond the musical and satirical levels, the perspicacious reader will perhaps begin to discern the ideal meaning which, while paramount, destroys neither the musical nor the satirical levels. The combination in a single fragment or verse of all three aspects leads to symbolism . . .

Moscow,
26 September, 1901.

# INTRODUCTION

The name of Andrei Biely (1880-1934) is at last beginning to become familiar to Western readers. Some sixty years ago the critic D. S. Mirsky declared that if Alexander Blok was the greatest of writers belonging to the Russian Symbolist movement, then "certainly the most original and influential was Biely". He went on to declare that "he is perhaps the greatest Russian humorist since Gogol'...But it is a humour that disconcerts at first and is very unlike anything else in the world. It took the Russian public some twenty years to learn to appreciate it, and it will hardly take the uninitiated foreigner by storm."[1] In fact, the monoglot Anglo-American reader's "initiation" into *any* aspect of Biely's art did not begin for another thirty-five years or so, when a US publisher finally plucked up the courage to issue John Cournos' deeply flawed but pioneering translation of his greatest novel, *Saint Petersburg*. It took a writer and critic of Valdimir Nabokov's authority, however, to gain Biely a permanent niche in the Western reader's pantheon of world literature, which he did in the mid-1960s by declaring unambiguously that Biely's novel was one of the four greatest works of twentieth-century fiction (Kafka, Proust and Joyce collected the other honours).

Since then the doubts of potential translators and publishers alike seem to have vanished. English versions of Biely's two other great novels, *Kotik Letaev* and *The Silver Dove*, appeared in 1971 and 1974 respectively. Robert Maguire and John Malmstad produced their monumental retranslation of *Petersburg* in 1978, while his *Collected Short Stories* and *The First Encounter*, his greatest poetic work, appeared in English the following year. With the decision of Penguin Books to reprint the Maguire/Malmstad *Petersburg* in their Modern Classics series at the end of 1983, Mirsky might well have concluded that the English-reading public at least had finally been "taken by storm".

Born in Moscow in 1880, at a time when the great age of Russian Realist fiction was coming to an end, Biely was to become in the decade and a half preceding the 1917 Revolution the leading exponent of experimental,

1

"modernist" fiction in Russia. His early work, and particularly his four prose *Symphonies* published between 1902 and 1908, constituted a complete break with the *formal* traditions of Realist fiction which had dominated Russian literature over the previous sixty years. To quote a recent Soviet book on the subject: "Biely was the most audacious reformer of Russian prose, renouncing all its achievements and canons in the most demonstrative fashion in his search for new formal possibilities... There are not even distant analogues to Biely's *Symphonies* in the past history of Russian literature."[2] It was this generic peculiarity, the exceptional nature of the attempt to appropriate "musical form" to literature, that Biely highlighted in his foreword to the *Dramatic Symphony* and which was his reason, indeed, for writing those prefatory remarks. The reader has no very clear idea about how the work is to be read. Is it prose? If so, then what is he to make of its segmented structure, its exaggerated rhythm, its simplified syntax, its leitmotival repetitions? Is it poetry? If so, it looks like prose, has no obvious first-person narrator and deals with imagined characters and events. It is a hybrid, in fact, made up of both poetic and prosaic elements, and this apparent complexity of narrative purpose and formal embodiment may be the reason why translators have fought shy of rendering the *Symphonies* into other languages. As far as I am aware, only the *Third Symphony (The Return)* has been published in any language other than Russian—Czech and Japanese versions appeared in 1964 and 1971 respectively—and the *Dramatic Symphony* has never been translated at all, apart from isolated fragments in works of specialist literary criticism.

Biely's real name was Boris Nikolayevich Bugayev. He was the son of Nikolay Vasil'yevich Bugayev, a famous mathematics professor at Moscow University. In his memoirs, Biely tells us that he began to write in the autumn of 1896 when he was sixteen years old. "I wrote a great deal," he said, "but I kept it to myself... There was an endless epic poem in the manner of Tasso, and a fantastic tale featuring an American yogi who could kill somebody merely by looking at him. And lyric fragments, too, quite feeble, but with a hefty dose of 'home-grown' decadence (I hadn't done any reading yet)." Like most very young writers, he turned to prose fiction without any fixed idea about the kind of thing he wanted to write. Nor did he have any firm views on the way Russian literature was developing. Not unlike Alexander Blok at about the same period, Biely became aware of "the new literature" only after he had already begun to write it himself. Indeed, according to an autobiographical note written in 1933, the year before he died, Biely's creative interests did not begin with literature al all. Music was his first love, and it was through music that he

2

came to poetry and prose. "I felt more of a composer than a poet," he wrote. "Music long overshadowed the possibility of a literary career for me, and I only became a writer by accident...Had circumstances turned out differently I might have become a composer or a scholar." Elsewhere he tells us that in the late 1890s he felt himself at "the meeting-point of poetry, prose, philosophy and music. I knew that each was defective without the others, but as to how to combine them all within myself, I had no idea. I hadn't sorted out whether I was a theoretician, critic and propagandist of art, a poet, a prose-writer or a composer. But I could feel creative forces welling up within me, telling me that I could achieve anything and that it was up to me to form myself. I saw my future as a keyboard, and it depended on me to play a symphony."

Piano improvisations expressing his own most cherished feelings and aspirations soon went hand in hand with the writing of poetry and lyric prose. Indeed, his first literary efforts actually arose, he tells us, as "attempts at illustrating those youthful musical compositions of mine." At about the same time, towards the end of 1896, he also read Arthur Schopenhauer's *magnum opus*, *The World as Will and Representation* (1819), for the first time. This philosopher's monistic view of the force underlying the universe, the World-Will, blindly renewing itself at all levels of existence and into eternity without any possibility of transcendence, made an enormous impression on the young Biely, and the first part of his *Dramatic Symphony* is imbued with negative imagery inspired by Schopenhauer's work. An example is to be found in the opening fragment.

> All were pale and over everyone hung the light-blue vault of the sky, now deep-blue, now grey, now black, full of musical tedium, eternal tedium, with the sun's eye in its midst.

But it was not just the philosopher's metaphysical pessimism which came to his notice. Biely was equally impressed by Schopenhauer's irrationalist theory of aesthetic cognition, and particularly as it related to music. "I had always loved music," he tells us in his memoirs, "but once I had mastered Schopenhaur's musical philosophy, I increased my attention to the art threefold. And music began to speak to me in a way it never had before."

It was Schopenhauer's contention that through music man gains access to the deepest forces underlying the universe: he is able to contemplate the noumenal Will itself. This metaphysical assertion lies at the basis of Schopenhauer's hierarchical classification of the arts, in which music is supreme. For music, unlike poetry, painting, sculpture and architecture, is "quite independent of the phenomenal world ... It is a copy of the Will itself . . . For this reason the effect of music is so very much more powerful and penetrating than is that of the other arts, for these others speak only of the shadow, but music of the essence of things." Biely accepted this account of music's metaphysical grandeur wholeheartedly, as we can see from statements which he made over a number of years. "Better than any other art, music is able to express the eternal," we read in a diary entry for July, 1899. "And the eternal is closest to us and most accessible in music." While in a letter to his friend Emile Medtner of August, 1902, he actually referred to music as "so to speak, the equivalent in this life of the next world". Signs of Biely's glorification of music — and of his disapproval of anything tending to impair its effect — occur throughout the *Dramatic Symphony*.

Not surprisingly, in view of his subsequent attempts to transfer musical techniques to literature, there was at least one important area in which Biely disagreed with Schopenhauer, and that was in respect of art synthesis, particularly the way in which music and poetry might interact. According to Schopenhauer, music was the highest art form and had no need of support from any of the others. Programme music or "painting in sounds" was particularly to be condemned, as was grand opera. "When music joins too closely to words and seeks to mould itself to events," he wrote, "it is attempting to speak a language which is not its own." This total rejection by Schopenhauer of the notion of the *Gemsamtkunstwerk*, or synthetic art form, was something that caused Wagner a good deal of trouble in his time, and the same was true of Biely at the end of the century. Biely's most thorough-going attempt to grapple with this problem at the theoretical level was his first significant published article "The Forms of Art", which appears in English for the first time in this present volume. His most successful attempt at exploring the problem in artistic form was the *Dramatic Symphony* itself, which happened also to be his first published *creative* work.

Although a great deal of Biely's mental energy in the last years of the century was spent in theorising, it will come as no surprise to discover that he had no firm ideas about what he was actually doing when he wrote his first prose *Symphonies*. "Their structure arose by itself," he wrote in 1907, "and I had no clear idea about what a 'symphony' in literature should be." He had definite ideas about the nature of "symphonic music", however. "Programme music is not the sublimest thing which the art has to offer," he wrote in his diary in 1899. "In terms of purity and directness of effect it is far inferior to non-programmatic music. This is why, when we listen to a symphony, we do not attempt to discover why it was was written or what it

4

is supposed to represent. For in a symphony we contemplate the sum total of all possible images in a given connection, all possible combinations of events which come together to form a vast and fathomless symbol . . . This is why symphonic music is infinitely higher and purer than operatic music." The empirical reality was rather different, however. "I used to dream of programme music," he admitted many years later. "The subjects of my first four books were drawn from musical leitmotifs . . . " Symphonic music might occupy its noumenal realm unsullied by the arts beneath it, therefore, but other musical forms were open to interpenetration, and able themselves to influence the writing of literature. In particular, Biely was attracted by the orchestral suites and lieder of Grieg and by Wagner's *Der Ring der Nibelungen* during 1899.

The first substantial prose piece of Biely's to be specifically associated with "musical form" was the work which he later referred to as his *Pre-Symphony*. He began work on it early in 1899 and had completed it by the autumn of that year. It was a manifestly immature piece of writing, and Biely apparently destroyed the final version five or six years later. An earlier, unrevised redaction has survived, however, and was published in the Soviet Union in 1981. Between December, 1899 and July, 1902 Biely went on to produce four more *Symphonies*. The first of these, the so-called *Northern* or *Heroic Symphony* took him a year to write and was completed during December, 1900. The *Second* or *Dramatic Symphony* was composed in rapid bursts between March and July of the following year. The *Third Symphony, The Return* was written between November, 1901 and August, 1902, partly overlapping with the first version of the *Fourth Symphony*, which was completed in June and July of the latter year. They were not published in the exact order of composition, however. As I have already said, the *Dramatic Symphony* was Biely's first venture into print and preceded the *Northern Symphony* by fifteen months or so. A few extracts from the *Fourth Symphony* appeared in a Moscow miscellany during 1903, but the rest of the work was never published in its original form. Biely made a number of frenzied efforts to rewrite it over the years that followed, and it was eventually published as *The Goblet of Blizzards* in April, 1908, having been completed eleven months earlier. Meanwhile, *The Return* had appeared as a separate volume at the very end of 1904.

It was fitting that the *Dramatic Symphony* should have been offered to the public before Biely's other works, since it embodied better than any of them the themes which would engage his attention over the next few years and the literary strategies he would develop to express them. In this respect, it was quite different from the other Symphonies which are less complex in their way, less adventurous, less full of possibilities for the future. Large claims have been made by critics over the years concerning the *formal originality* of the Symphonies as a whole and their importance in the context of Russian literary history. The Formalist critic Viktor Shklovsky, for example, was of the opinion that "without the Symphonies modern Russian literature would have been impossible,"[3] and his words have been echoed by others. "Whatever we may think of Biely's *Symphonies* as artistic achievements," writes the critic Glebe Struve, "they must be viewed as significant experiments, foreshadowing important developments in modern prose fiction."[4] "These first works of Andrei Biely opened up a whole epoch in the development of the twentieth-century experimental novel," says another recent critic, Léna Szilárd.[5] And so it goes on. In certain respects these claims are difficult to justify, however, for the works in question are not homogeneous achievements. The novelty of the *First* and *Third Symphonies* is largely superficial, for example, and certainly a lot less striking than many commentators have been willing to admit. While the *Goblet of Blizzards* was, in its way, a monstrous aberration, a true *ne plus ultra* based on a fundamental misapprehension of the semantic possibilities of verbal art. The *Dramatic Symphony* was a genuinely open-ended experiment, however, and when critics attempt to substantate their claims concerning Biely's early formal originality, it is invariably to this, his *Second Symphony,* that they turn for convincing, concrete illustrations.

Biely wrote the first part of his *Symphony* in March, 1901 when he was half-way through his second year of study at the Physics and Mathematics Faculty of Moscow University. A brilliant student, he threw himself into the study of the natural sciences, while at the same time developing his growing interest in art, religion and philosophy. It was not just Schopenhauer who interested him now. He had become fascinated with the writings of Nietzsche, and especially *Thus Spake Zarathustra* which he described in his memoirs as being at one time his "bedside book". It was the style of the work that particularly attracted him (Nietzsche himself referred to it as a "symphony"). But he also admired the philosopher's courageous determination to overcome the metaphysical pessimism of Schopenhauer and affirm the value of the individual's existence in *this* world, since, in his opinion, there was no other. However, if Biely was taken with Zarathustra's creative moral stance ("So live that you must wish to live again"), it was not because he accepted Nietzsche's denial of any metaphysical sanction. On the contrary, Biely believed firmly in the existence of a transcendent realm and, like so many others at the turn of the century, he looked to the imminent enactment of events foretold in the Revelation of St. John the Divine. The struggle between monistic views of the universe on the one hand and dualistic faith in transcendence on the other would form the main philosophical "sub-text" of the *Dramatic Symphony* itself.

The Bugayev family had long been on friendly terms with their neighbours, Mikhail Sergeyevich Solov'yov and his wife, Ol'ga Mikhaylovna. Biely spent a great deal of his time at their apartment during the late 1890s, discussing recent developments in European art and literature and also religious questions, seen mainly from the Orthodox point of view. Their son, Sergei, was to become one of the greatest friends of his youth. Mikhail Solov'yov's elder brother, Valdimir Sergeyevich, was Russia's most famous philosopher, and although Biely met him on several occasions, it was their final discussion in May, 1900, two or three months before Solov'yov died, that made an indelible impression on the young student. Vladimir Solov'yov had not long finished writing what was to become his most famous work, the *Short Story of the Antichrist*, in which he described in great detail the way in which the events foretold in Revelation would be played out in the modern world. The Antichrist would come, tempting people to spiritual destruction, but would at last be vanquished as the woman clothed with the sun appeared in the heavens and Christ descended again to his people, resurrecting the dead and reigning with them for a thousand years. Solov'yov's tone was utterly serious. "Taken in general," he wrote, "this story presents a series of conjectures of the probable based on the actual facts. Personally, I believe this probability to be very near the certainty, and I am not alone in this belief."[6]

Biely was undoubtedly one of the believers (he had written part of a mystery play entitled "The Antichrist" himself, long before he met Vladimir Solov'yov), but no less than the philosopher he was aware of the danger of "false prophets", of too hasty a search for signs of God's intervention. All the same, he greeted the new century in 1901 filled with hope and expectation—expectation that the events long prophesied would finally begin to play themselves out on earth — and he looked to the sky over Moscow for signs. And not just to the sky.

The *Dramatic Symphony* is very close to the thoughts and feelings which Biely experienced himself during what his friend Medtner would call that "years of dawns". In his "Material for an Intimate Biography" written some twenty years later, Biely remembered that he had experienced the very things that his hero Sergei Musatov was suffering, and in this respect the *Symphony* could be seen as a ''random extract, almost a factual record of the real and immense symphony" which he lived through during the first few months of 1901. It was full of real events and people. Some identities were more or less transparently hinted at in the work itself. Others were concealed, so that we have to rely on Biely's own testimony to decipher their biographical significance. Many of the more interesting or famous prototypes are mentioned in the notes to the present translation. Some of the more anecdotal ones (for example, the ''real-life" counterparts of Musatov's brother, Pavel, or the "aristocratic old man") have been omitted. Apart from Sergei Musatov, however, whom Biely considered to share traits both of himself and Sergei Solov'yov, there are two other characters who deserve individual comment, namely the woman referred to as the ''fairy-tale" and her secret admirer, the "democrat".

In his "Intimate Biography" Biely recalls a concert which he attended in February, 1901. It was a performance of a symphony by Beethoven. What made it particularly memorable was that it was the first time he caught sight of Margarita Kirillovna Morozova, the beautiful wife of a wealthy Moscow businessman and Maecenas. Thereafter he would often see her at similar occasions, but he never attempted to introduce himself to her. He did, however, write her a series of anonymous letters. Here is an extract from the first of them, written early in 1901:

A man who died long ago to ordinary life may be forgiven a certain boldness. He, for whom the world is becoming an illusion, has greater rights. He, who has discovered a second reality in life, is beyond its laws. . .

We all experience the twilight . . . But does it betoken sunset or dawn? Do you know nothing of the great dawn sadness? Dawn illumined turns everything upside down; it places people as it were beyond this world. The sorrow of daybreak — that, and that alone, has called forth this letter . . .

What is close becomes distant, what is distant becomes close. Not believing what you cannot understand, you become filled with loathing for that which you can. You sink into a symphony of dreams . . .

Do you know nothing of the great dawn sadness? . . .

We said farewell to philosophy . . . We bowed down to the ground before Nietzsche. We thought that a giant was towering on the horizon; the two horns of the moon appeared above his head; they melted the giant: it was only the deep-blue cupola of a cloud; he melted away in the evening sky before the astonished eyes of his worshippers . . .

In vain we awaited the *New Jerusalem* which always seems on the point of descending from the heavens, but never does so. Neo-Christianity has deceived us . . .

The sun did not arise, the twilight was not extinguished . . .

But everything changed . . . I found a living symbol, an individual banner, all that I had sought but which had not yet had time to be accomplished,

You — my future dawn. In You are the events to come. You are the one emblazoned with the sign! Do you know this?...

When I approached the furthest reaches of the abyss, "there appeared a great wonder in heaven; a woman clothed with the sun, and the moon under her feet, and upon her head a crown of twelve stars." (St. John the Divine). The mystery was revealed.

You are the emblazoned one! Do you know this?...

Prayer and genuflection!

Every person has several *raisons d'être*. He is both himself, and a symbol, and a prototype. I do not need to know you as a person because I have got to know you better as a symbol and I have proclaimed you as a great prototype...

You are the Idea of the philosophy of the future!...

Your cavalier.

In another letter sent later that year he actually referred to her as "my fairy tale, my happiness. And not mine alone." Like the character in his *Symphony*, Margarita Kirillovna did not take these letters amiss, although, as she explained in a memoir written much later, it was some time before she discovered his true identity. "In the spring of 1903," she wrote, "I bought a little volume of the poet Andrei Biely in a bookshop: *The Second, Dramatic Symphony*, since I had heard about it from a lot of people. When I got home, I opened the book and was startled to find that it contained expressions taken word from word from the letters of this 'cavalier', and I realised that it was me he was talking about in the *Symphony* under the name of 'fairy-tale'." Life and art were not always such perfect replicas of each other, however, and unlike the hapless "democrat", Biely did not commit suicide through unrequited love. He spread his complex personality and experiences far and wide throughout the work.

Biely wrote Part One of the *Symphony* in March 1901 almost as a transcript of his day to day impressions in the Arbat district of Moscow. He would read it aloud to Mikhail Solov'yov and his family every day at tea. The second part was written that May within the space of twenty-four hours over Whit Sunday and Whit Monday and is redolent of the white lilac which, he says in his memoirs, was growing outside the windows of his parents' flat on that white night. Parts Three and Four were completed the following June and July at his mother's estate in the country. To Biely's surprise, Mikhail Solov'yov insisted that it should be published as quickly as possible and brought it to the attention of Valery Bryusov, the self-proclaimed leader of the Symbolist movement in Moscow. Bryusov was very positive about the work and explained that his publishing house,

Scorpio, would be delighted to take it on, but that there was not enough money available to ensure immediate publication. Solov'yov offered to pay for it himself. And so the *Dramatic Symphony* was offered to the public the following April, although not under the writer's own name. Professor Bugayev had become Dean at Moscow University by this time, and the son wanted to spare his father the embarrassment of being associated with such a "decadent" work. Eventually, Mikhail Solov'yov came up with the name Andrei Biely (Andrew White in English), a successful invention considering the symbolic significance of what Biely called the "white elements" in the work as a whole. Thus the writer was launched.

The "plot", if we can call it that, of the *Dramatic Symphony* is a complex affair, because Biely appears to go out of his way to disrupt the reader's conventional expectations that events and characters will develop coherently. It is this aspect of the work that has led many critics to comment on its "experimental" character, in particular the way it anticipates similar structural displacements in later "modernist" fiction by Joyce, Zamyatin, Musil, and so on. The Russian critic Askol'dov was one of the first critics to analyse this aspect of the *Symphony*. "The first thing that strikes you," he wrote, "is the absence of a firm plot line . . . The first few pages are a fairly incoherent succession of different descriptions and images . . . There are ten or twenty plots succeeding one another in a confused way without beginning or ending."[7] Was it possible to unify this apparent chaos of impressions and events? Askol'dov thought that it was, and he did so by following the co-ordinates of the narrator's implied angle of vision above and beyond the phenomenal world to a point where the confusion and purposelessness of earthly life were resolved in a higher, cosmic or spiritual purpose. It was Biely's great achievement, said Askol'dov, to embody the "symphonic" harmony which exists between the phenomenal and noumenal worlds.

Askol'dov was certainly right to point to the author's attempt to unite the *Symphony*'s kaleidoscopic themes and variations at a higher level of meaning. But the actual significance of that symbolic concord, or rather the way it is arrived at, was more complex than the critic cared to admit. Is it really the case that the narrator's intimations of cosmic harmony in the world beyond are a sufficient resolution of the many this-worldly disharmonies which appear to be the primary theme of the *Symphony*? This is not an easy question to answer, and since for the most part Biely succeeds in avoiding direct authorial comment in the work, the key to its symbolic significance beyond the empirical plane is likely to be found in the author's handling of one of its most striking structural features: its system of repeated images or leitmotifs, what he called in his own foreword — "musical phrases".

As we have already seen, the first series of leitmotifs to be introduced— on the theme of metaphysical boredom or *ennui* — is decidedly negative. The anonymous narrator looks around at the apparently pointless labours of so many nameless, isolated individuals scurrying around the Moscow streets and comments: "All were pale and over everyone hung the light-blue vault of the sky ... None knew where they ran to or why, fearing to look truth in the eye." The motifs here and elsewhere embody the implied author's negative philosophical concern with the theme of "eternal return", the possibility despondently raised by Schopenhauer and joyfully affirmed by Nietzsche, that there is no ultimate reality beyond that of the life-force itself, that the only transcendent truth is that there is not transcendence and that mankind has nothing to hope for except an eternity of meaningless repetitions of the phenomenal world. The chief consolation offered by Schopenhauer was that man could in some sense escape the pain of his subjection by retreating into the abstract contemplation of it, or by creating patterns of meaning within the charmed circle of art. This at least, he supposed, was better than nothing.

Biely disagreed with the philosopher on this point, however, regarding his suggested remedies as passive, quietistic, and even as "Buddhist". Art might redeem the world, but not in the metaphorical sense which Schopenhauer appeared to have in mind. Art must be "theurgic". It must awaken men to the reality of the spiritual forces at work in the universe and enable them to transform their lives accordingly. Art needed, therefore, to focus on the experience of people who were struggling to make deeper sense of a world resolutely opposed to the possibility of transcendence. The notion of "eternal return" and various ways in which it might be philosophically resisted, are therefore *tested* in the plot and characterisation of the *Dramatic Symphony*. And the chosen instrument of that "testing" is the work's principal hero, Sergei Musatov.

Musatov does not figure in the *Symphony* until half way through Part Two (he is not *named* until half way through Part Three), but from the moment of his appearance the work begins to acquire a much more traditional and coherent plot structure, as the narrator concentrates on revealing to us the nature of the hero's apocalyptic beliefs. This is done first by direct reporting of a prophetic speech which he makes at a gathering of mystics and other intellectuals in the capital. "The Third Kingdom is now dawning," says Musatov, "the Kingdom of the Spirit... Now we shall have to suffer the terrible final battle ... The time of the four horsemen is

11

dawning: the white, the red, the black and the pale rider of death . . . This was the mysterious thought of Dostoyevsky. This was the heart-rending cry of Nietzsche . . . I hear the thundering of a horse's hooves: it is the first rider." And there would be delivered a man who "is to rule all nations with a rod of iron . . . His mother is the woman clothed with the sun." Although the narrator does not comment directly on Musatov's speech, it is ironised more or less overtly in the pages that follow, as motif after motif is systematically taken up in the plot and debunked. Many of Biely's most humorous effects derive from this juxtaposition of high seriousness and absurdity. A little boy is seen playing with some other children in a Moscow courtyard, for example. The narrator describes the "austere and thoughtful" expression on his face and the way in which his eyes concentrate the deep blue colour of the sky. One hand is grasping a metal piston and he suddenly begins to belabour his little sisters with this "rod of iron". They begin to scream and throw fistfuls of sand at this "despot" of theirs. The boy meanwhile wipes the sand from his face with an inflexible gesture full of significance, looks up at the turquoise sky and leans on the metal rod. Then he suddenly throws it to the ground, jumps down off the pile of sand and rushes out of the courtyard, whooping with joy as he does so.

The mystical notions thus mocked are not necessarily to be regarded as completely devalued in the implied author's eyes, however. For, although numerous other "negative" satirical characters receive short shrift in this *Symphony*, the narrator lavishes a great deal of attention on its hero and shows us more and more of the mental and emotional difficulties under which he is labouring. In particular, we become aware that he is both tortured and tempted by recurring images of the "eternal return". Part Three is given over almost completely to a description of Musatov's visit to the countryside, where he hopes to make sense of the different metaphysical beliefs at war within him. While there he seems to hear a voice saying: "Everything returns . . . Everything returns . . . All is one . . . all is one . . . in every dimension. Travel to the west, and you will return to the east . . . The essence of all things is contained in the visible world." And this refrain is then echoed in the sound of the trees around him. The narrator does not say so, but the real reason underlying Musatov's manic espousal of naive Apocalypse à la Vladimir Solov'yov may be the urgent need he feels to silence these siren voices within him.

Musatov struggles very hard against what he feels instinctively to be a potent and seductive force for evil within him, that of philosophical nihilism. For the most part the battle takes place below the level of consciousness and surfaces in the form of occasional leitmotifs concerning the "eternal return" and, of course, in his fanatical desire to assert the imminence of events foretold in Revelation. It is only when his eschatological dreams finally collapse (the person whom he had taken to be the "woman clothed with the sun" turns out to be an ordinary society lady and her "man child, who is to rule all nations with a rod of iron"—a little girl dressed in boy's clothes called Nina), it is only after all this that the kaleidoscopic view of reality prevalent before Musatov's appearance on the scene reasserts itself, now at least partly motivated as a reflection of the hero's emotional collapse. He then appears to be the victim of an extraordinary hallucination, a scene which, with its depiction of mundane reality about to succumb to some nameless metaphysical threat, looks forward to the writings of Kafka. "*They* pointed out the open door to him. He heeded *their* advice. Don't blame him, esteemed readers! It was *they* themselves who whispered to him: 'Here you will resolve your misunderstanding'." He enters a room "just like any other government office" where he encounters a fat, red-nosed, red-haired man seated on the floor in white underclothes and a nightcap. In bursts a lean, menacing creature named Petrushka, or variations on the same, who begins a bizarre conversation with Musatov on the nature of truth:

> "Could this really be the world of the fourth dimension revealing itself to me?" thought Musatov...
> "Yes, yes, yes, yes, yes!" prompted the essence of things in the shape of Petrushka. "A million times yes! This is the so-called world of the fourth dimension!...The point is that it doesn't exist at all..."
> "But is there anything behind the wall!" whispered Musatov, who had turned deathly pale.
> "Just such a room with just such wallpaper as you'll see in any government office, with just such an eccentric as yourself hammering at the wall with his fists, thinking there is something on the other side..."

Soon after this Musatov departs in terror. The narrator remains, however, and goes on to describe how the two occupants of the room actually grow horns before his eyes. Are they agents of the forces of darkness? As if to back up his suggestion that such forces actually exist, the narrator switches to the Novodevichy Convent and shows us the figure of the recently deceased philosopher, Vladimir Solov'yov, who has taken to appearing on the roofs and in the cemeteries of Moscow, often accompanied by Bars Ivanovich, a friend of his from the other world. "I think, gentlemen, that you would have glimpsed two figures sitting on the graves;" says the narrator, although of course, "perhaps I only thought I saw this, gentlemen," he adds a little later. In other words, he does not *insist* on a supernatural interpretation. He is willing to allow the reader to reach his own conclusions about the events and experiences he has described.

On the other hand, the *Symphony* is far from being devoid of dogmatic elements. There is a second network of "positive" leitmotifs running through the work—apple blossom, white lilac flowers, sunsets, the image of a nun dressed all in black tending the graves at the Novodevichy, etc.—and it is elements like these which critics like Askol'dov have in mind when they write of the *Symphony* as expressing and ideal of cosmic harmony. These motifs are associated with a small group of relatively unironised characters like the arch-priest Ioann and a "passive and knowing" individual called Petkovsky. They also eventually embrace the democrat's and subsequently Musatov's "fairy-tale". What all these figures have in common, we come to realise, is their instinctive awareness that human love will eventually overcome the forces of evil and that the day prophesied by St. John the Divine will not, after all, be long in coming. The *Symphony* ends with a scene set in the Novodevichy Convent the following spring which is obviously intended in some sense to neutralise the effect of the "eternal return" motifs by integrating them ("and again, and again") with the positive images from the second series. The result was evidently meant to be a scene of some lyric and mystical power. (see pages 157-8).

In a sense this structural "resolution" of the work's dissonant themes is rather spurious, however, being little more than the implied author's attempt to impose a harmonious ending from above. We feel Musatov's travail from within and this is perhaps the *Symphony*'s greatest achievement, but we are told about the fairy-tale's inner serenity from without. (This is even truer in the case of the black nun who is silent throughout the work.) Either Biely's "positive" theme about religious faith and the ability of human love to defeat the sense of purposelessness and evil so well embodied elsewhere in the *Symphony*, is not translated into character and action at all (this is the work's *lyric* dimension), or, where Biely does make the attempt, the results rarely rise above the level of flaccid sentimentality. Musatov encountered genuine resistance from surrounding reality: the "positive" characters do not. The "negative" dimension of the work is perhaps a greater imaginative achievement than the apparently "positive" side, although it was, of course, the lyrical, theurgic message associated with the fairy-tale and Father Ioann that was more attractive to Biely, as biographical author. Emile Medtner suggested as much in an early review, and, Biely tells us in his memoirs, "I joyfully agreed with him."

Roger Keys

1. DS. Mirsky, *A History of Russian Literature*, London, 1949, book 2, pp. 463-4. Originally published as *Contemporary Russian Literature, 1881-1925*. London, 1926.
2. Ekaterina Starikove, "Realizm i simvolizm", in *Razvitie realizma v russkoi literature*, vol. 3, ed. U. R. Fokht *et al.*, Moscow, 1974, p.196.
3. V. Shklovsky, "Andrei Biely", *Russkiy sovremennik*, No. 2, 1924, p. 243.
4. G. P. Struve, "Andrej Belyj's Experiments with Novel Technique" in *Stil- und Formprobleme in der Literatur*, ed. P. Böckmann, Heidelberg, 1959, p.467.
5. E. Silard (Szilárd), "O strukture Vtoroi simfonii A. Belogo", *Studia Slavica Hungarica*, 13, 1967, p. 311.
6. V.S. Solov'yov, *Tri razgovora, Sobranie sochinenii*, vol. 10, Saint Petersburg, p. 89.
7. S. Askol'dov, "Tvorchestvo Andreya Belogo", *Literaturnaya mysl'*, Al'manakh 1, Petrograd, 1923, p. 74.

# THE DRAMATIC SYMPHONY

*Translated by Roger and Angela Keys*

## PART ONE

1. A season of sweltering grind. The roadway gleamed blindingly.

2. Cab-drivers cracked their whips, exposing their worn, blue backs to the hot sun.

3. Yard-sweepers raised columns of dust, their grime-browned faces loudly exulting, untroubled by grimaces from passers-by.

4. Along the pavements scurried heat-exhausted intellectuals and suspicious-looking citizens.

5. All were pale and over everyone hung the light-blue vault of the sky, now deep-blue, now grey, now black, full of musical tedium, eternal tedium, with the sun's eye in its midst.

6. Streams of white-hot metal poured down from the same spot.

7. None knew where they ran to or why, fearing to look truth in the eye.


1. A poet, writing a poem about love, was having difficulty with the choice of rhymes. And dropped an ink-blot, and, turning his eyes towards the window, took fright at the tedium of the sky.

2. The grey-blue vault smiled at him with the sun's eye in its midst.


1. Two men were arguing over a cup of tea about people great and small. Their cracked voices had grown hoarse with debate.

2. One sat with his elbows on the table. He raised his eyes to the window. He *saw*. He broke all threads of the conversation. He had caught the smile of eternal tedium.

3. The other was leaning his short-sighted, pock-marked face towards his antagonist, spattering him with spittle, as he finished bawling out

19

his objection.

4. But the other did not bother even to wipe his face with a handkerchief; he had withdrawn into the depths, plunged into the fathomless.

5. And the victor threw himself back in his chair, his good-natured, stupid eyes peering out at the silent one through golden spectacles.

6. He knew nothing of the removal of the final veils.

7. And in the sweltering streets, in the blinding whiteness, men in dark-blue jackets drove by on water-carts.

8. They sat on barrels which gushed out water underneath.


1. High buildings towered like a spread of bristles, puffed up like fattened pigs.

2. One moment they would wink their countless windows at the timid pedestrian, the next they would flash him a blind wall as a sign of contempt, then they would sneer at his hidden thoughts with belching columns of smoke.

3. On these days and at these hours documents and memoranda were being composed in offices, and a cockerel led hens around the paved courtyard.

4. Two grey guinea-fowl were in the courtyard too.

5. A talented artist had painted a "miracle" on a large canvas,[2] and twenty skinned carcases hung in the butcher's shop.

6. And everybody knew this, and everybody concealed it, fearing to turn their eyes towards the tedium.

7. And yet there it was, shadowing everyone, a misty, invisible outline.

8. Although the water-cart men were consoling each and everyone by spreading mud everywhere, and children bowled hoops along the boulevard.

9. Although the light-blue vault laughed into everyone's eyes, the terrible, grey-blue vault of the sky with the sun's eye in its midst.

10. Which was where they came from, the austere and cheerless songs of sovereign Eternity. Eternity supreme.

11. And these songs sounded like scales. Scales played from the world invisible. Always the same and the same. Just as they finished so they began again.

12. Just as they soothed, so they began again to disquiet.

13. Always the same and the same, without beginning or end.


1. Day was fading. A military band played on Prechistensky Boulevard, nobody knew why, and inhabitants of buildings and basements had come to the boulevard, nobody knew from where. They walked up and down the boulevard. They crowded in front of the band, pushing and jostling one another.

2. They cracked jokes and stood on ladies' hems with bears' paws. And the man with the baton carried on waving and waving. The trumpeters with knitted brows strained every nerve: "Laugh, Pagliaccio, at your broken love, laugh that your life is poisoned fore'er."

3. A pale, bilious-looking hunchback, with a bandage hiding one cheek, promenaded to the music, beside his anaemic wife and little lame son.

4. He wore a yellow overcoat, flame-red gloves and a huge top-hat. He was a doctor from the city hospital.

5. He had only yesterday consigned to the mental asylum a certain consumptive who had suddenly revealed the abyss to the whole hospital.

6. As he did so, the madman continued to whisper quietly: "I know thee, Eternity!"

7. Everyone was terrified to hear the hidden secret. They summoned the hunch-back doctor and sent the crazy man where he belonged.

8. That had happened yesterday, and today the hunch-back doctor promenaded to the music beside his anaemic wife and little lame son . . .

1. In a fashionable shop a lift was operating. The operator of this mechanical diversion spent his time frenziedly flying up and down between the four floors.

2. Everywhere crowds of men and women tried to burst their way into the little box, crushing and cursing each other.

3. Although staircases had been set in the same place.

4. And over this crush an expressionless voice of majesty and mystery proclaimed from time to time: "The account."


1. A handsome youth stood before a bookshop window in a shabby double-breasted jacket, his neck inordinately dirty and his fingernails black.

2. Pulling at his chin, he looked sentimentally at a copy of a German translation of the works of Maksim Gor'ky.

3. Standing in front of the bookshop were a pair of fast carriage-horses. Sitting on the coach-box was a perspiring driver with a noble face, black moustache and beetling brows.

4. He was like a second Nietzsche.

5. A fat pig with a snout for a nose and dressed in a smart overcoat pranced out of the shop.

6. It grunted, seeing a pretty lady, and indolently skipped into the carriage.

7. Nietzsche touched the reins, and as the pig was borne off by the horses, it wiped the sweat from its brow.

8. The student stood before the bookshop window a little longer and went on his way, trying to maintain his independent air.


1. There were many more horrors yet . . .


1. It was growing dark. In the east a dark-blue haze was imbued with the mist of sorrow and the tedium of eternity, and the sounds of an orchestra drifted over from the boulevard.

2. As if everyone had thrown the weight of tedium from their shoulders, and little boys and girls were running up and down the streets with bunches of forget-me-nots.

3. You would meet at that hour, in every direction, dispirited bicyclists. Dripping with sweat, backs bent, legs working away. With rolling eyes they would ring their threatening bells as they overtook one another.

4. At that hour a philosopher was returning home with affected gait, carrying the *Critique of Pure Reason* under his arm.

5. Coming towards him in a cab was a bowler-hatted gentleman with a tufty red beard.

6. He sucked the handle of his walking-stick and hummed a jolly music-hall tune.

7. They exchanged bows. The philosopher touched his peaked cap with an affectedly offhand gesture, and the passenger in the cab parted his lips, revealing his rotten teeth, and twirled his hand in greeting.

8. He was no genius, but his father had been known for his intellect . . .

9. And the place where they had honoured each other with salutations, became empty . . . To the right could be seen the philosopher's back and the spine of the *Critique of Pure Reason,* and to the left could be seen the cab-driver's bent frame as he urged his jaded horse to bear the passenger away.

10. And over this empty place mournful sounds emanated from an open window: "A-ooo, a-ooo."

11. It was a singer from the Conservatoire trying out her voice.


1. The philosopher rang the door-bell. And when the door was opened, he hurled the *Critique of Pure Reason* onto the table and fell onto the bed in a state of objectless tedium.

2. His last thought had been as follows: "Kant without Plato is a torso without a head." He had fallen asleep and appeared headless in his thoughts.

3. And the bust of Immanuel Kant standing on the desk shook its head reproachfully and stuck out its tongue at the sleeping philosopher.

4. The philosopher slept. And above him the shadows thickened, forever the same and the same, austere and gentle, relentlessly dreamy.

5. Eternity herself wandered the lonely apartment, tapping and laughing softly in the next room.

6. She sat down in the empty armchairs and adjusted the portraits beneath their covers.

7. The bookshelves were casting sharp shadows and the shadows met, and, as they did so, grew thicker . . . As if they were hiding in the dark.

8. But no-one was there except Immanuel Kant and Plato who were standing on the desk in the form of half-length busts.

9. Kant was complaining to Plato about the young philosopher's slowness of mind, and the philosopher slept at the hour of evening twilight with a pale, ironic face and compressed lips . . . And a little child could have smothered him.

10. After the hot day a cool breeze was blowing through an open window and meandering around him.

11. Coming in through the open window were the sounds of something soft being beaten. The inhabitants of the basement floor were beating the dust out of their furniture, which they had dragged into the courtyard.

12. And he woke up. And his first thought concerned the impossibility of uniting the teachings of Kant and Plato. And he raised his tired head from the crumpled pillows. And he shivered from the evening cold.

13. And staring him straight in the eye was the moon, sharply outlined against the dark-blue enamel of the sky . . . A red moon.

14. He jumped up in terror and clutched at his head. Like someone crazed by love, he stared at the circle as it grew paler.

15. If somebody from outside had looked in at him through the window, his face would have seemed a fearful thing, pale, enshadowed and tired.

16. Forever the same and the same he appeared on days of the full moon in spring.

17. His nerves were playing tricks and so he turned to the Valerian drops.


1. And in the next room an enormous mirror reflected forever the same thing.
2. *There* was the horror of absence and non-existence.
3. *There* the *Critique of Pure Reason* was lying on the desk.


1. It was midnight. The streets were deserted.
2. A certain street ran past a sleepy river. Four little side-streets led down to the river.
3. These were First Conception Lane, Second Conception Lane, Third Conception Lane and, finally, Fourth Conception Lane.
4. In the sky someone seemed to be playing eternal finger-exercises. Someone was striking one note and then another.
5. First the one, and then the other.
6. A little man with a pince-nez on his elongated nose minced along the deserted pavement lit up by street-lights.
7. He wore galoshes. He carried an umbrella under his arm, although it was dry and warm.
8. In his hands he held a folio volume. It was the life of a saint.
9. He walked silently, floating past like a shadow.
10. No-one knew where he came from, and no-one could say where he would end up.
11. On the other side of the street a window opened and from inside certain individuals approached it.
12. Two women with impassive, pale faces. They were thin and wore black mob-caps.
13. They were dressed in black. The elder one pointed impassively at the passer-by, observing: "Popovsky."

14. And Popovsky was already walking by. No power on earth could say where he would end up.

15. There was a desperate tedium. In the sky someone was playing eternal finger-exercises. It seemed as if someone was striking one note and then another.

16. First the one, and then the other.

17. Just as it finished, so it began again.


1. The street led into the square. Popovsky was already wandering through the square.

2. In the square a paraffin street-lamp smoked.

3. If you stood facing the moon you could see a huge, black column of soot above the lamp.


1. That night an apartment was burgled. Two crooks from the Khitrovsky market broke open the locks, but went off with a pair of old galoshes for the lack of anything more profitable.

2. In the morning the sun had not yet risen, but the paving-stones already began to radiate white. The cab-drivers had not yet sallied forth. No pedestrians disturbed the silence.

3. There was a bright absence of people.


1. People slept in basements. People slept in attics. People slept in bed-chambers. Rich and poor, clever and stupid — all slept.

2. Some slept in ugly, contorted positions, some slept with their mouths open. Some were snoring. Others looked dead.

3. All slept.

4. In the ward of a mental hospital people slept just like the healthy ones. Only one particular melancholic paced up and down past the hospital beds, troubled with colic.

5. He shrugged his shoulders as he bent his pale, ironic face down

towards the stupid, animal features of those who were asleep. Suddenly he covered his face with his hands, and burst into peals of soundless laughter.

6. He shouted out in a cracked voice: "Inescapably they sleep and eat! They get undressed just to cover themselves with a blanket and become insensible! Inescapably they put foreign objects into their mouths!"

7. "What do they do?"

8. But at this point violent stomach pains cut short his lucubrations. His brows contorted.

9. A threatening ray of sunshine pierced the window-frame and bathed his dry, demented face with its scarlet light.

10. And as if seized by foreboding, he raised his long, thin, threatening finger towards the window where the pink light of morning was bursting in.

11. Where the healthy slept just like the sick.


1. Popovsky was a conservative. Free thinkers hated him for his free attitude to their opinions.

2. Lucid minds contorted their browless foreheads before his puny little figure.

3. He had the effrontery not to fear blank cartridges, and real ones flew over his head, as Popovsky was rather short.

4. Popovsky was a man of the church. He shunned the devil and progress. He thought that we were living through our final days and that whatever shone with talent came from the Devil.

5. He detected signs of devilry in his acquaintances and read the Gospel in the evenings.

6. Popovsky was a cynic. His thin lips were always twisted in a scarcely perceptible smile. He was on the look-out for the ridiculous in every opinion and rejected everything.

7. Such was Popovsky, and no power on earth could change him.

1. During the morning Popovsky had been doing the rounds of his acquaintances to tell of his erudition.

2. He wore galoshes and carried a redundant umbrella under his arm.

3. Horse-drawn trams dragged along in varous directions, and the grey-blue vault of the sky shone, the terrible, tedious sky with the sun's eye in its midst.

4. Above the misty city someone played eternal finger-exercises. And tedium, like a dear, familiar image, danced on the seven hills.

5. And there . . . above . . . someone passive and knowing, day in, day out carried on repeating: "Pigsty."

6. The same thing he repeated day in, day out.


1. At that hour, as he left for the hospital, the pale, bilious-looking hunchback tied a bandage over his cheek: his teeth ached.

2. He did not tie it very well. Two little ears stuck up over his head.

3. And once again someone who *knew* said impassively: "Pigsty", and the cockerel in the paved courtyard seized its opponent by the comb.

4. Then everything slipped out of place, everything broke away, and there remained the . . *fathomless*.


1. And the moments passed. Pedestrians succeeded each other like moments . . . And every passer-by had his moment of walking along over every place.

2. Everyone did everything at a certain time. There was not one capable of doing without time.

3. And time passed unceasingly, and the passing of time carried the reflection of misty Eternity.


1. By mid-day Popovsky had made the rounds of five places and in five places had spoken about five subjects.

2. In one place he developed his ideas about the dangers of analysis and the advantages of synthesis.

3. In another place he expressed his view about the Apocalypse.

4. In a third place he said nothing because everything had been said. Here he played a game of chess.

5. In the fourth place he spoke of earthly vanity, and in the fifth place he was not received.

6. Little Popovsky hung his head and proceeded to the sixth place.


1. On the main road Popovsky met his enemy, the democrat.

2. The latter was smartly dressed. His gloved hand gripped a scarlet rose.

3. Popovsky was on the way to his desired discussion on parish church schools, and the democrat sauntered with walking-stick in hand.

4. They exchanged mutual contempt. They exchanged bows. Only yesterday the democrat had showered Popovsky with abuse at the office of a liberal newspaper.

5. And his Excellency, a solid, liberal editor, purple and respectable, had added his own sharp words to the democrat's.

6. This was what they called keeping abreast of the century

7. That was yesterday . . . And today the democrat strolled the streets with scarlet rose in hand, pointing timid, dreamy eyes towards the sky.

8. Already he was forgetting Popovsky. The light-blue stared down at him, one and the same for liberals and conservatives.


1. Then the men on the water-carts drove past, carrying on the struggle with the dust.

2. Impassive people seated on barrels.

3. Water poured abundantly from underneath the barrels, filling the streets with redundant liquid and spreading mud everywhere.

4. And the moments passed. Pedestrians succeeded each other like moments . . . And every passer-by had his moment of walking along over every place.

5. And every barrel became empty at a certain moment. The man was driving to fill it.

1. And then the democrat saw his fairy-tale, the democrat's fairy-tale.

2. A carriage proceeded down the street and seated on the coachbox was the inert top-hatted driver, waving an English whip.

3. Seated in the carriage was the fairy-tale, the democrat's fairy-tale.

4. She had coral-coloured lips and blue, deep-blue eyes, the eyes of a fairy-tale.

5. She was the wife of a good-natured sea-centaur who has had civic rights since the time of Böcklin.[3]

6. Once he used to snort and dive amidst the waves, but then he conceived the idea of changing his marine ways for life on dry land.

7. He exchanged his four hooves for two feet, then dressed himself in a tail-coat and became a man.

8. Her husband was a centaur, but she herself was a fairy-tale and sea-nymph.

9. Thus passed the fairy-tale, the democrat's fairy-tale, with the hint of a smile at her dreamer as she fixed him with her deep-blue gaze.

10. After spattering mud on a respectable-looking old gentleman dressed in an old overcoat.

11. The respectable-looking old gentleman shouted and made threatening gestures at the fairy-tale as she flew away. He wiped his mud-drenched face and hissed: "The devil take the rich" . . .

12. And he continued on his way to the office of the *Moscow Gazette*, bearing his editorial.

13. The democrat, elegant and spruce, derided its conservatism to his heart's content.

14. But that was the next day . . . Now he was lost in daydreams, scarlet rose in hand.

15. And he saw nothing, and he heard nothing. Remembering his fairy-tale, smiling at the image of the blue-eyed nymph.

1. In a huge shop selling everything fashionable the lift worked diligently, and the man in charge of this mechanical diversion flew frenziedly between the four floors.

2. Even as he berthed at the first floor, people were already waiting on the second with stupid, impatient faces. Just as he berthed at the second, a murmur of indignation rose from the ground floor.

3. Amidst all this uproar mysterious voices could be heard here and there proclaiming: "The account."


1. On the basement floor a canary chirped. This was where a shoe-maker worked, contemplating the feet of pedestrians as they flashed by.

2. Boots passed by with a squeak, as did yellow shoes. The absence of any boots passed by.

3. All this was seen by the crafty shoe-maker, and he cheerfully twirled his awl, piercing some fresh leather.

4. And along the railway line from Ryazan' hurtled a goods train full of Cherkassy bulls. The bulls thrust out their sleepy muzzles and the steam engine shrieked like a lunatic.

5. It was full of malicious and exultant glee as it hauled the trainload of bulls towards the city abattoirs.

6. And everybody knew this. And everybody was afraid to look truth in the eye. And there she stood, tedium, lurking behind everyone, revealing in the midst of life's trivialities the fathomless.

7. And the desperate man who had turned to face her suddenly submitted to her threatening finger.

8. She was all the more terrible on a bright, sunny day.


1. The sea-centaur drove past, the one who has had civic rights since the time of Böcklin.

2. His good-natured, corpulent silhouette exuded elegant simplicity.

He was being borne away by black horses.

3. He was *thinking* . . .

1. The young philosopher was reading the *Critique of Pure Reason*, sitting in a rocking-chair and rocking himself with his feet.

2. One moment he would be lost in reading, the next he would drop the book onto his knees and strike his head against the back of the rocking-chair as he thought over what he had read, improvising philosophical tricks and psychological jokes.

3. So, after reading about time and space as *a priori* forms of cognition, he began to think whether he might not fence himself off with screens, concealing himself from both time and space, escaping from them into the fathomless distance.

4. At that moment everything was torn away, every string, every thread was broken off, and smiling into his eyes was the light-blue vault of the sky, now deep-blue, now grey, full of musical tedium, with the sun's eye in its midst.

5. And he stopped reading. He approached the enormous mirror hanging in the adjacent room. He looked at himself.

6. Before him stood a pale young man, not bad looking, with hair tousled above the forehead.

7. And he poked his tongue out at the pale young man as if to say to himself: "I am mad." And the young man answered him back in kind.

8. So they stood in front of each other with gaping mouths, each supposing that the other was a fake.

9. But who could say for sure?

1. To distract himself he approached the broken piano. He sat down on the stool and opened the lid.

2. And the piano began to disclose its lower jaw so that the individual on the stool could strike its teeth up and down.

3. And the philosopher struck his old friend's teeth up and down.

4. And blow followed blow. And the philosopher's servant stuck cotton-wool in her ears although she was in the kitchen and all the doors were closed.

5. And this horror was an itch in the fingers and was called *improvisation*.

6. The door to the next room was open. There was a mirror there. Reflected in the mirror was the back of an individual on a stool in front of a broken piano.

7. Another person sat and played just like the first. Both sat with their backs to each other.

8. And so it continued to infinity . . .


1. But the doorbell rang. And the philosopher, having closed the lid of the piano, went into the next room.

2. The room was empty. Only the *Critique of Pure Reason* lay on the table.

3. The woman who entered was dressed in black and she glanced impassively at the *Critique of Pure Reason* after propping her thin, wrinkled face against her gloved hand.

4. Her hand held a handbag . . . The sun was already sinking. Its fiery whiteness was turning to gold . . .

5. Down below someone had a tooth extracted.


1. But the philosopher entered, having combed his hair, and graciously invited his guest into the drawing room

2. The drawing-room furniture was covered in dust-sheets. The black guest sat side on to the massive mirror. She was a relative and began to speak of her sad circumstances.

3. Her son had died. She had buried him today. Now she was alone in the world.

4. She had nobody. Nobody needed her.

5. She received a pension. She had been dressed in black for ten years already.

6. This was what she said. No tears fell from her eyes.

7. And her voice was the same as ever. A stranger might have thought he glimpsed a fleeting smile upon her lips.

8. But it was sorrow.

9. She related the tale of her son's death in the same tone in which she had ordered luncheon the day before; and two days ago she had complained about the expense of groceries in the same way.

10. She was already accustomed to sadness. Events both trivial and crucial called forth the same feeling inside her.

11. She was quiet in her grief.

12. She had already finished and was sitting with lowered head, fingering her bag with her gloved hands.

13. And he stood before her in an affected pose, cleaning his nails and saying: "You must look at the world from a philosophical point of view."

14. But the doorbell rang. He asked her to wait as you do with relations and hurried out to meet his guest . . .


1. Popovsky stood in the next room holding a copy of *The Lives of Saints Cosmo and Damian* under his arm.

2. They shook hands. They began to speak as if they were both angels.

3. Innocently smiling, they discussed the state of the weather . . . Then they fell silent . . . Then the philosopher struck the *Critique of Pure Reason* with his hand and said: "There's one place here . . ."

4. And everything went smoothly.

5. Soon Popovsky twisted his thin lips. This signified that he was a cynic. Soon he began to look around to see if the Devil was there. This signified that he was a man of the church.

6. And his antagonist, with beautifully affected gestures, walked up and down the room, deducing Schopenhauer from Kant.

7. Soon everything became confused. All that could be heard were fragmentary exclamations: "The postulate . . . the categorical imperative . . . the synthesis . . ."

8. . . . And . . . in the next room the black guest sat displaying her profile to the massive mirror.

9. She awaited her host as you do with relations and frequently blinked her tiny brown eyes.

10. She could understand nothing. Only snippets of sentences reached her.

11. And next to her in the mirror sat another woman just as black as she was.

12. So she gave up waiting for the philosopher and left, as you do with relations, without saying goodbye.

13. As she put on her galoshes, she said to the servant: "But my Petyusha has died."

14. She had no thoughts . . . She could still hear the loud voice of the parish deacon ringing in her ears: "Grant unto him eternal rest."

15. Such was the stentorian deacon.


1. The philosopher spoke long. He spoke fervently. He spoke to the point of exhaustion, until Popovsky went away.

2. Tired and pale he went to his room and fell down on the bed.

3. His last thought was as follows: "It's wrong, it's wrong . . . Once again it's all wrong . . . Oh, if only I could hide! Oh, if only I could find rest!"

4. He slept . . . And above him the shadows thickened. Forever the same and the same, austere and gentle, relentlessly dreamy.

5. Eternity herself in the shape of a black guest wandered the lonely rooms, sitting down in the empty armchairs, adjusting the portraits beneath their covers, in an eternal way, as you do with relations.

6. The bookshelves were already darkening, and the shadows met and, as they did so, grew thicker.

7. Thus he slept during the spring twilight with a pale, ironic face and no trace of affectation . . .

8. And a little child could have smothered him.

9. His window was open. From there a cool breeze was blowing in.

10. Looking at his window from the window opposite was fat Dormidon Ivanovich who had come home from the office.

11. Dormidon Ivanovich was drinking tea from a saucer and, as he looked out at the window opposite, thought: "It would be interesting to know how much they pay for that flat."


1. Once again the dispirited bicyclists appeared, once again forget-me-nots were on sale. And on another boulevard played "Laugh, Pagliaccio".

2. Standing at the intersection of two streets was an apparently respectable family-man, decently dressed and with a grey moustache.

3. There was nothing loud in his appearance. Everything conformed, everything was subordinate to the general idea.

4. He was smoking an expensive cigar as he discussed a commercial venture. His enormous nose hinted at Armenian origins.

5. He was a visiting crook from the southern provinces.

6. And, like a crook, scurrying towards him was a Moscow University professor, leaving the examinations.

7. Neither of them knew why they existed or where they would end up. Both were in the position of pupils who had written extempore essays but who did not know what mark they would receive.


1. The moon was rising. Again, as yesterday, it was rising.

2. So it would rise tomorrow, too, and the day after tomorrow.

3. And after that it could not avoid its inescapable waning.


1. The philosopher awoke . . . He raised his head from the crumpled pillows . . . And staring him straight in the eye was the moon, sharply outlined against the dark-blue enamel of the sky . . .

2. A red moon! . . .

3. The philospher jumped up in terror and clutched at his head. Like someone crazed with love he stared at the terrible disc.

1. At that moment the democrat was writing a critical article in his room. He caught sight of the moon. He gave a sorrowful smile.
2. He abandoned his pen and his thoughts, which jumped and squirmed about like fretful puppies.
3. He rubbed his forehead and whispered: "It's wrong, it's completely wrong."
4. He remembered the fairy-tale.

1. . . . A silk curtain was raised. Somebody had opened a window at the other end of the city.
2. The house was extremely fashionable and decadent, and in the window stood the fairy-tale.
3. She adjusted her red hair and smiled as she looked at the moon. "Yes . . . I know," she was saying.
4. She stared with deep-blue, sorrowful eyes, remembering her dreamer.
5. By the entrance black horses stood and waited for her, because it was the time for taking a drive.

1. At that moment the pale, bilious-looking hunchback had finished his lunch, after returning from the hospital.
2. His cousin had come to visit him, bemoaning his sufferings. He said that in the evenings he thought objects were shifting from their places.
3. The hunchback patted his highly-strung cousin on the shoulder and remarked in a good-natured way that this was nothing to worry about, just a case of "Dr. Kandinsky's pseudo-hallucinations."*
4. As he finished speaking, he opened the piano and began to play Beethoven's *Pathétique Sonata*.

*See Korsakov's *Psychiatry Course* (Author's footnote)

5. But the highly-strung relation could not bear it. The highly-strung relation thought that objects were shifting from their places.

6. Just a case of Dr. Kandinsky's pseudo-hallucinations.

7. But the hunchback continued to play the *Pathétique Sonata*. His eyes were merciless. Two little ears stuck up over his head.

8. He was a great sentimentalist.

9. And the sounds poured forth . . . The lame son paused in his examination preparation . . . He shed a few surreptitious tears.

10. The servants were already asleep. The lights had been put out in the servants' hall although the official time for sleeping had not yet arrived. The pale, bilious-looking hunchback's mother-in-law stood at the door of the kitchen.

11. Her enormous stomach and pig-like face shone in the play of moonbeams.

12. She swore like a fishwife as she heaved up the slumbering cook.


1. That night Popovsky walked along Ostozhenka Street.

2. No-one knew where he came from, and no power on earth could alter his path.

3. On the other side of the street two pale women in black opened the window.

4. The elder pointed impassively at the passer-by and said in a colourless voice: "Popovsky."

5. Both were sorrowful, as if they had lost a son. Both resembled each other.

6. The one was like the mirror-reflection of the other.


1. A window was open in the decadent house and at the window the silhouette of a Böcklin fairy-tale fleetingly appeared.

2. The fairy-tale walked aimlessly up and down the room and a dark sorrow seemed to cloud her face.

3. "Tedium!" she said at last. She sat down in an armchair.

4. And far away, far away, as if to mock the world, someone began to shout for help. There was a sound of whistles blown in alarm.

5. One man had smashed another man's nose because they were both drunk.


1. That night everyone slept. Morning came with slanting sunny rain.

2. The sun chuckled merrily through the pouring streams. The water-cart men were null and void for a whole half-day.

3. That morning they buried a typhus patient at the church of St. Nicholas-on-Chicken-Legs. His faded, lilac coffin, adorned with gold tinsel, was borne out of the church.

4. Walking ahead of it was the ginger-bearded priest with a red nose.

5. Three wagonettes were following on behind, all dilapidated. They clattered aimlessly along the intractable roadway.

6. The first was adorned with faded blue upholstery, the second with faded red, and the colour of the third was impossible to make out.

7. It was very sad. It lacked only a barrel organ and a clown.

8. The people sitting in the first wagonette were crying.

9. The people sitting in the second one only had sad faces.

10. There were two old women sitting in the third with satisfied, plump faces. One held a plate wrapped in a kerchief.

11. This contained consecrated cake.

12. The two old women indulged in a lively chat, anticipating the funeral feast.

13. There and then in that very procession sat one individual already infected with typhus, who would take to his bed the next day.

14. So the mourning procession made its way toward the distant cemetery.

1. The streets were being dug up all over the place. There were people with animal features, some laying stones, some sprinkling sand on the stones, some ramming the stones into the ground.

2. Lying to one side was a pile of rags, of sheepskin coats, of caps, of thick slices of bread and a yellow dog, asleep as usual.

3. And in the spot where yesterday a foul-smelling beggar sat displaying his imitation ulcer to impassive passers-by, today they were boiling asphalt.

4. Fumes were everywhere. The asphalt-men would spend several minutes hanging from metal harnesses to stir the black soup in the vats.

5. Then they would pour the black soup onto the pavement, sprinkle sand over it and leave it to cool by itself.

6. The tired passers-by scurried around this acrid spot, hurrying no-one knew where.


1. The person reading the *Critique of Pure Reason* was on form today.

2. He had found some errors in Kant and constructed an original system on their foundation.

3. He rummaged among philosophical works on his bookshelves, raising unspeakable clouds of dust.

4. And on the other side of the street Dormidon Ivanovich's window was closed since Dormidon Ivanovich himself was sitting in the Revenue Department.

5. He was the head of a section. The clerks loved him.


1. The dreamy democrat positively could not work. Yesterday he had written a letter to his fairy-tale nymph and today she should be receiving it.

2. He was commissioned to write a critique of a certain conservative work. He was showering the conservative writer with caustic remarks as was only right.

3. But his own thoughts seemed to him to be as tedious as dogs. The pen slipped from his hand.

4. And laughing and joking straight in his face was that blue purity. He looked at the window dreamily.

5. What was it he had been doing?



1. The blue-eyed nymph had received a letter from the dreamer. She was in a state of agitated uncertainty.

2. She had spent the whole day looking in contempt at the good-natured centaur, making nasty remarks to him.

3. The centaur would straighten his collar and shout at the servants.

4. He was a good-natured centaur. He felt oppressed by nasty remarks.

5. Once he used to snort and dive amidst the waves, but now everything was quite, quite different.



1. The aristocratic old man was giving a party. On Fridays there would be carriages standing outside the entrance to his house.

2. Both scientists and diplomats appeared at his parties as well as people of the highest society.

3. He was a good-natured old man and did not stand aloof from fashion.

4. Conservatives, liberals and Marxists all loved the aristocratic old man equally.

5. Even the great writer, ploughman and count would come here without any hostility.[4]

6. The good-natured old man with the star on his chest would pat everyone on the shoulder and say equally to each: "Yes, yes, of course" . . .



1. In the elegant drawing-room the corpulent wife of the important old man showered the guests with compliments.

2. The guests were dressed in tail-coats and white ties. They were all

pleasantly at ease and guilelessly graceful. They all emitted rays of light and had no inkling of it as they shone.

3. All of them, having passed through the three stages of transformation, had become children. There were no savage lions or clumsy camels to be met with.[5] This happened not because the old altruist did not like them.

4. It happened because the rigorous servants would not admit everyone without exception.

5. The old man's two young daughters twitched their shoulders as they asked the guests: "Would you like some tea?"

6. Many accepted, but others said no. These were invited to go into the hall.

7. In the hall well-groomed and effeminate young men in tail-coats talked pleasant nonsense to each other.

8. Young girls, beautiful and ugly, took up their nonsense and carried it to the point of absurdity.

9. All were cheerful. No-one was bothered about anything.

10. The Kingdom of Heaven appeared to have come down to earth.


1. The aristocratic old man himself, clean and shaven with a star upon his chest, would take first one, then another of his guests under the arm and lead him off to his study.

2. This was no ordinary study but a room filled with expensive copies of the great masters.

3. The old man would sit each one opposite him in just the same way and say pleasant things to all of them.

4. He would begin a clever conversation with each, and whatever was talked about, the subject would resolve itself simply and easily.

5. The diplomat agreed with the old man's views. The old man showed the careerist portraits of powerful people personally signed by them.

6. He praised science to the scholar and once wept on a student's breast in pity for the youth of today.

7. To the cynic he showed uncensored Paris editions, after locking the door beforehand.

8. The good-natured old man loved everyone and tried to do good things for each.


1. The moon was rising. Again, as yesterday, it was rising. So it would rise tomorrow, too.

2. And after that it could not avoid its inescapable waning.


1. Popovsky's teeth ached.


1. Trampling the soft carpets as he did so, the democrat, elegant in his tail-coat, walked up the main staircase.

2. As he entered the drawing-room, he was nearly knocked off his feet by two tail-coated, smooth-chinned youths. One of them was carrying a guitar.

3. They charged towards the hall from where the sound of music drifted and where people young and old were being spontaneous to the accompaniment of a grand piano.

4. The smooth-chinned youths said *"pardon"* in French and careered on crazily past the democrat.

5. As he entered the drawing-room the democrat nonchalantly inclined his perfumed head to express his elegant esteem for one and all.

6. He spent more time listening than speaking. That was what propriety demanded of him.

7. After all he was a critic, and silence became him.


1. Amongst the guests was a young man with a long nose and sweaty hands. A fashionable musician.

2. A talented artist was there, too, who had a depicted a "miracle" on a large canvas.

3. A philosopher acquaintance was there as well, because he was talented.

4. An important individual from conservative circles was there, too, who had connections with affairs of the press.

5. The important individual complimented the brilliant democrat. With a pleasant gesture of his hands and an agreeable laugh the individual remarked in a velvety voice: "The difference in our opinions doesn't prevent us from appreciating each other."

6. And the brilliant democrat inclined his perfumed head to express his utter impartiality.


1. The aristocratic old man was not here himself. He sat in his study with a philanthropic old prince.

2. Nodding their shaven old faces towards each other, the old men talked about all this modern nonsense.

3. The benefactor-prince regretted the abolition of serfdom, and the obsequious host chewed sympathetically away with his toothless mouth, inserting "Yes, yes, of course" into the words of the prince.


1. The fairy-tale entered the drawing-room with soft, silent steps.

2. She wore a light grey dress embroidered with pale silver leaves. A diamond star glittered in her red hair.

3. Quietly and softly she trod as if concealing her elegance with artlessness.

4. The height of aristocratic naturalness.

5. And the young democrat paused in mid-sentence, and felt the ground give way beneath his feet.

6. And behind the fairy-tale nymph the outline of her centaur already grew, his head merging into his neck, his neck into his shirt, and his shirt into his tail-coat.

7. "I think everyone here knows everyone else," said the hostess, and then, remembering, introduced the fairy-tale to the democrat.

1. They offered each other their hands, and the democrat felt the gaze of her deep-blue eyes transfixing him.

2. The gaze was affectionate. The democrat realised there was no anger over the letter.

3. Sounds of the piano reached them from the hall where elegant youth gave itself up to refined pleasure.

4. And they spoke to each other artfully, pleasantly, in cloyingly genteel phrases, as if nothing were the matter.

5. Although the democrat's every word had an unspoken accompaniment, and the accompaniment signified: "It's all wrong, it's all wrong."

6. The Böcklin fairy-tale attended his tinsel speech with playful sympathy and the occasional "really?" or "well, how interesting!"

7. But this "how interesting" concealed the answer to "it's all wrong": "Yes, yes . . . I know . . ."

8. An elegant, mischievous game not without cunning.


1. "Do you like music?" the fairy-tale asked the democrat, and in response he said: "No, I don't" as if with the accompaniment of three asterisks.

2. And the three asterisks meant: read as follows: "I like music better than anything else in the world after you."

3. And the fairy-tale replied: "I suppose a serious man like you would not have time for music," with another three asterisks.

4. And the three asterisks meant: read as follows: " You really aren't at all stupid, you know."

5. Then the fairy-tale turned to the dumpy hostess and said with friendly ease: "You'll attend the festival of flowers, of course?"

6. But at this moment the resplendent old man's elder daughter appeared in the doorway and, pointing her tortoise-shell lorgnette in the democrat's direction, invited him to join their jolly company.

7. He lowered his head reluctantly and followed this skinny young lady, realising that *this* would please the blue-eyed nymph.

8. In the hall young men and women talked pleasant nonsense to one another.

9. In their midst the philosopher was gloomy: he had seen the moon in the window entwined in haze and had withdrawn into the fathomless, threatening distance.

10. He had discovered dreadful errors in his new system. The infallibility of the *Critique of Pure Reason* appeared as an aggravating blot in his spiritual field of vision.

11. His nerves were playing tricks.


1. The stout centaur — simple and refined — sat down next to the talented artist who had painted the "miracle".

2. He wanted to buy the "miracle", but for now was patiently listening to a speech on the inconveniences of oil painting.


1. In the hall there was singing. A clean-shaven youth in a tail-coat played the piano.

2. He jigged on the edge of his stool, with hands raised over the keys, and elbows bearing the whole weight of his body.

3. This was the accepted thing.

4. A good-natured military man from the General Staff with silver aiguillettes played the guitar, keeping time with his soft, lacquered boots, nodding his greying head to right and left.

5. So they pleasantly amused themselves. The Kingdom of Heaven appeared to have come down to earth.


1. The young democrat sat, lulled by the gypsy tune and his conversation with the fairy-tale.

2. He listened to the singing as if enchanted.

3. The singer was the soldier from the General Staff with a black moustache and a pleasant but dull-witted face. "Beneath your enchanting caress," he sang, pronouncing his r's like a Frenchman, "I

come back to life once more . . . Once more I cherish former dreams, once more I long for love and pain . . ."

4. He had a deep, passionate voice and muffled the ends of his words like a true gypsy.

5. And the chorus of young men and women joined in: "Give me oblivion with a kiss, heal the torments of my heart!! Send doubt away and heal me with a kiss!!!"

6. The young men and women swayed their heads to right and left, the accompanist jigged on the edge of his stool, and the host's elder daughter, as thin as a rake, screwed up her eyes as she sang, tapping the deft accompanist with her tortoise-shell lorgnette.

7. The young democrat, looking at the singers, thought: "These are not people, but the representations of my happiness," and the old man's daughter nodded at him, as if to say: "We are representations, but not people." And the resplendent old man himself, clean and shaven with a star upon his chest, stood in the doorway, an affectionate smile on his face as he watched the young people singing and said in a scarcely audible whisper: "Yes, yes, of course" . . .


1. The philosopher frowned. A storm-cloud had covered the moon in the window. He had found another error in his speculative constructions.

2. One of the tail-coated youths leaned over towards the old man's daughter and said of the philosopher: *"Qui est ce drôle?"*

3. The soldier from the General Staff with the black, cockroach moustache and the pleasant, good-natured face was singing: "Ruthless reason tells me time and time again, that you will cease to love me, that you will betray me! But I do not flinch from the fetters of your charms: the power of your beauty enslaves me!!"

4. He had a deep, passionate voice and muffled the ends of his words like a true gypsy.

5. The chorus joined in. The young men and women swayed their heads to right and left, the accompanist jigged on the edge of his stool. The young democrat thought: "These are not people, but the representations of my happiness." The old man, clean and shaven

47

with a star upon his chest, stood in the doorway, an affectionate smile on his face as he watched the young people singing and said in a scarcely audible whisper, "Yes, yes, of course."

1. At this moment the democrat saw the fairy-tale and her centaur moving in the distance towards the staircase that led to the exit.

2. She looked towards the hall with that strange, wandering gaze of hers which proves nothing, and gave a sad smile with her coral-coloured lips.

3. Then he caught a fleeting glimpse of the fire of her hair. Then the democrat realised that they were never likely to meet again at such close quarters.

4. And once again strings snapped and everything collapsed. And tedium beckoned from the chaos, tedium, eternal as the world, dark as night.

5. Tedium stared from the window, from the eyes of the horrified philosopher.

6. Something appeared to change. Someone entered who was not there before. Someone familiar and invisible stood in the over-bright, over-lit hall.

7. And the soldier from the General Staff, noticing nothing, carried on with the end of his song: "Even though my fate for that ecstatic moment should chance to be the grave . . ."

8. "The grave," thought the democrat. The chorus joined in. The young men and women swayed their heads to right and left. The accompanist jigged on the edge of his stool.

9. And the democrat saw that these were all false representations, and the shaven old man with the star on his chest approached him affectionately. He took him under the arm and whispered: "I keep abreast of the century. I love the young people of today."

1. The democrat and the philosopher, blacker than the night, walked out onto the street together.

2. A thunderstorm was drawing near.

3. They were heading in the same direction, but they walked in silence, listening to the eternal finger-exercises.

4. Moment succeeded moment, always the same from time immemorial. The two rows of street-lamps flickered their tongues of gas.

5. The young democrat, listless and sad, envisaged the old man standing before him, nodding derisively. The philosopher's nerves had finally splintered. Madness crept up on him, slowly but surely.

6. It already stood behind him. He was afraid to turn round suddenly and see its threatening face.

7. Thus they walked through the dark night, doomed to destruction.

8. Already the dust moved along the sleepy streets, a whirling cloud.


1. At the crossroads they took their dry farewell. Despite all, they remembered that they belonged to different parties.

2. The philosopher walked with affected gait down a lonely lane, afraid to turn around.

3. He thought that some threatening horror was following him, and he remembered the enormous mirror in his lonely flat and that at this moment his room was reflected in the mirror.

4. He was troubled as to whether the reflection was accurate.

5. Then he walked up to the entrance. The reverberant door slammed shut behind him.


1. A stranger wearing a worn peaked cap was walking down the stairs. The neurotic young man trembled like an aspen leaf. His face snuffed out like a lamp without oil as he glimpsed in the stranger's features the seal of awful predestination.

2. The stranger lowered his eyes as he walked down the stairs. And as he walked past him, the nerve-racked philosopher thought: "Any moment now he'll look at me! . . ."

3. He thought that at that moment "It will all end."

4. But the person in the peaked cap did not raise his eyes. He gave a hazy smile and ran from the staircase. Then the reverberant door slammed shut behind him.

5. But the neurotic young man could not recover from the terror that had passed. He still kept thinking it might return at any moment.

6. And the door opened again. Someone ran up the stairs.

7. And when the philosopher rang at his own door, the person who had entered was already approaching the upper landing.

8. It was the postman. Ringing at the next door.


1. And then the door was opened for the madman, he did not look at the servant but walked on into his own room and locked it, afraid to let the threatening horror enter.

2. It was gloomy. A blinding flash of lightning split the darkness. A deafening crash of thunder shook the walls.

3. Hiding between the bookshelves of philosophical tomes was the pale stranger with the seal of awful predestination.

4. *This* was the threatening horror.

5. The reader of Kant gave a silent moan and crouched down on the floor.

6. He never rose from the floor again but took refuge under the bedstead. He wanted to escape time and space, conceal himself from the world.

7. My brothers, all really has ended for the man who has crouched down on the floor!

8. Somewhere a clock struck two. There was a flash of lightning. It did not illuminate the madman. He sat beneath the bedstead, smiling craftily at his plan.

9. Then the threatening horror emerged from behind the bookshelves with the philosophical tomes, opened the window and lowered itself down the drain-pipe.

1. And on the other side all was quiet and peaceful. The window in Dormidon Ivanovich's room was shut.

2. Dormidon Ivanovich himself snored quietly on his back. He dreamed that it was already Christmas and that he had received his bonus.


1. At that moment the young democrat shot himself without finishing the critical article which he was commissioned to write.

2. Placing the revolver to his temple, he smiled, remembering his fairy-tale, the democrat's fairy-tale.


1. And the fairy-tale, sad and dreamy, stood at the window of the decadent house, illuminated by flashes of lighting.

2. She held the democrat's letter. She was crying. Her coral-coloured lips formed a smile.

3. With a smile she remembered her dreamer.

4. And . . . there . . . in the distance . . . as if in mockery . . . the evening water barrels trundled along the streets.

5. These were false representations . . .


1. Popovsky's teeth ached. He was beyond good and evil, having forgotten both God and the Devil.


1. A white-haired elder looked out over the river. He leaned his elbows on the railings. His sorrowful face showed agonising horror.

2. At the foot of the hill a jolly coachman flew along, driving his pair of thoroughbred horses for all he was worth. The cheerful grooms were seated in the carriage.

3. In the distance the factories flickered with hundreds of flames.

4. Then the sorrowful elder raised his hands and said softly: "My God, my God!"

5. His reproach remained unanswered.

1. That night everyone slept. People slept in basements. People slept in attics. People slept in the house of the aristocratic old man.

2. Some slept in ugly, contorted positions, some slept with their mouths open. Some were snoring. Others looked dead.

3. All slept.

4. In the ward of a mental hospital people were also asleep. They slept just like the healthy ones.

5. It was already growing light. There was a joyless glimmer. The pale and cloudy day looked ominously in at the windows.

6. A cold, damp drizzle was falling.

7. But the day burst into flame, for all its gloom, and this seemed an appeal to the exhausted, an invitation to new pretence.

8. Only one mad melancholic was already sitting on his bed, staring impassively at those who slept.

9. A shiver ran down his spine. He felt nauseated. He felt nauseously subject to time.

10. He wanted to withdraw beyond the boundary of time, but did not know how.

11. And time flowed unceasingly. In the flow of time misty Eternity was reflected.

12. The melancholic said sorrowfully: "I know you, Eternity. I am afraid, afraid, afraid!"

13. And he lay down to sleep once again.


1. An express train hurtled down the tracks, dragging the sleeping Max Nordau to Moscow.[6]

2. Max Nordau snored in a first-class compartment, heading full steam for Moscow.

3. He was rushing to a conference of scientists and doctors.

4. All his life the zealous Nordau had struggled with degeneration. Now too, he had prepared a speech.

5. And the rain drizzled and beat against the windows of the compartment. The train hurtled along, dragging the sleeping Nordau across the mournful Russian lowlands.

1. In the morning the issues of three journals were published. The democrat did not manage to cast his eyes over them.

2. In the office of a liberal newspaper a purple-faced editor and a hungry poet talked.

3. The editor informed the poet that the democrat had shot himself out of civic sorrow, and the hungry poet promised to write a "strong" article "tearing to shreds" whoever deserved it.

4. Flags fluttered in the streets.

1. By mid-day the rain had stopped. The sun peeped out. Popovsky was doing the rounds to tell of his erudition.

2. He had made the rounds of five places and in five places had spoken about five subjects.

3. In one place he had spoken of the advantages of synthesis, in another he had talked about the Wanderers' exhibition.

4. In the third place he had played a game of chess, and in the fourth he had gauged the significance of the gnostics.

5. In the fifth place Popovsky was not received because the owner of the fifth place had already been taken off to the mental asylum that morning.

6. This was the philosopher who had become engrossed in reading Kant.

7. Pieces of paper were stuck on the windows of his flat, intended to signify that the flat was available to let.

8. Little Popovsky hung his head and proceeded to the sixth place.

1. It was six o'clock in the evening. The weather had cleared up. Dormidon Ivanovich was walking home from the office.

2. He walked past a tea and grocery shop. In the glass windows contented sausages were bursting.

3. Dormidon Ivanovich called in at the tea and grocery shop and wanted to buy himself a little bottle of cider to find out what the favourite drink of the French was like.

4. Dormidon Ivanovich was deliberately curious.


1. As he walked past the philosopher's former flat, Dormidon Ivanovich caught sight of the pieces of paper stuck on the windows.

2. Said Dormidon Ivanovich: "Ah! They're moving! Now it would be interesting to find out how much they pay for that flat!"

3. Then he went for a walk on the boulevard, leaning on his stick, good-humoured and fat.

4. The clerks jokingly called him Mastodon Ivanovich, but that was nonsense because he was not Mastodon but Dormidon.


1. The fairy-tale was buying some knick-knacks for herself. Crowds of ladies, young girls and men scurried from department to department.

2. The lift was working with all its might. The man in the little box spent his time frenziedly flying up and down between the four floors.

3. Here and there you could hear a metallic voice proclaiming: "The account."


1. That evening in a notable concert-hall a notable concert was due to take place, supplementary to the season.[7] A famous conductor had arrived. The whole of Moscow had bought itself a ticket.

2. As much as an hour before the concert a portly man was placing music on the music-stands, and ten minutes before the beginning those sitting in the front rows had assembled.

3. An impudent-featured man with unseemly side-whiskers had already arrived and sat in the fourth row.

4. This was Nebarinov, an indispensable member of social gatherings.

5. A countess had already arrived, and a princess, and the wife of a famous writer.

6. And a professor from the Conservatoire with a big beard but short hair, and a professor from the Conservatoire with a short beard but long hair, and a professor from the University.

7. And an aristocratic old man with his dumpy wife, and a gentleman with a beard but without a moustache, who loved Mendelssohn.

8. And the lawyer Ukho, and the young man Kondizhoglo, and many others who were all supposed to be there.

9. The centaur and his wife were certainly at the concert. The fairy-tale conversed with the chief of the City police who was talking nonsense in a pleasant way.

10. The chief of the City police was from the highest society. He joked and made insouciant remarks.

11. And the fairy-tale returned nonsense with nonsense, taking in the hall with her wandering gaze.

12. And an important personage had already entered her box. Then the famous conductor appeared.

13. Two people scurried up to present him with a flower garland.

14. And then it began . . . deepened . . . arose.

15. Just as it finished so it began again. Aways the same and the same, rising in the dispirited soul.

16. At this moment Nebarinov was looking around at the people present and remembering those who were not.

17. The centaur was attentive. The old man slept. His spouse would nudge him with her elbow and he would murmur as he woke: "Yes, yes, of course."

18. And, deeply moved, they nodded their heads in time, the countess and the princess and the wife of the famous writer.

19. The fairy-tale sat austerely outlined.

20. She was grieving.

1. And then it began . . .deepened . . . arose . . as if these were scales from an unknown world arising from no-one knew where and dying away again.

2. As if *this* was something independent and those blowing their trumpets and scraping their bows were something else . . .

3. As if the lights had grown dim. The notable concert-hall became small and constricted. Something broke off from something else . . . Became independent . . .

4. And the hall seemed strange and gloomy, and the lights flickered mournfully.

5. And the countless faces of the people listening looked like a spread of pale blotches against a black, fathomless background.

6. These faces were serious and austere, as if people were afraid to find themselves guilty of shameful weakness.

7. But *this* was stronger than all of them.


1. The sounds merged with the moments. A series of moments constituted time. Time flowed without ceasing. In the flow of time misty Eternity was reflected.

2. Eternity was like an austere woman dressed in black, peaceful . . . at rest.

3. She stood amidst those who were present. Each one could feel her icy breath behind his back.

4. She embraced each with her dark outlines, placed her pale, unearthly face against the heart of each one.


1. Like a great bird   . . . filled with sorrow. And the sorrow had no end.

2. This sorrow had travelled for thousands of years. Thousands of years lay ahead.

3. It had flown through all the planetary systems. And the planetary systems changed their direction.

4. And it was the same as ever, peaceful, majestic, ruthlessly dreamy.

5. Like a great bird. And its name was the *bird of sorrow*.

6. It was sorrow itself.


1. And amid the sharply outlined clouds the bright, waning moon was already visible. It had not fulfilled expectations and was waning ahead of time. It did everything not according to expectation but according to the calendar.

2. At this very moment it deceived Moscow, saying that it flew amidst motionless clouds.

3. But the opposite was the case.

4. Between the moon and the poor earth the clouds flew, nobody knew where from, nobody knew where to.

5. The North wind whistled and bent the young, tender trees.

6. In a restaurant window a drunken voice was bawling: "Cry! Cry! Do not hide your tears! . . . Cry! Cry! Cry! Do not hide your tears! . . ."


1. At that moment the express train arrived. Max Nordau jumped down from a first-class compartment.

2. The fearful Nordau eyed the platform, muttering in a scarcely audible voice: *"Die alte Moskau!"*

3. All around people scurried with suitcases, and the steam engine whistled like a mad thing.

4. And from somewhere or other far away you could hear the crazy cacophony of the Moscow cab drivers: "Come with me, sir, with me! Here's a cab . . ."

5. And Nordau was bewildered.


1. At that moment a white-haired old man dressed in a cap with ear-flaps and carrying an open umbrella, walked down the boulevard.

2. The street-lamps winked dully. Occasionally suspicious-looking individuals would pass by.

3. It was raining cats and dogs.

4. The white-haired elder paused and shouted out in a sorrowful voice, shaking his open umbrella: "My God! My God!"

5. A lone passer-by turned round in astonishment, hearing this cry . . . And the trees murmured as they bent over, beckoning into the uncharted distance.

# PART TWO

1. The moonlit nights gave way to moonless ones. A new moon was expected any day.

2. But for the time being there was no moon.

3. At the melancholy evening hour the roofs of buildings grew cold as did the dusty pavements.

4. Between the buildings there were open slits of sky. Walking on the right-hand side of a near-deserted by-street, you could see the tender yellow fading of the day, edged with smoky hulks of cloud.

5. A haze hung over Moscow.

6. In the near-deserted by-street a dwarf of an alms-woman, old, with a bluish pallor, walked towards the alms-house with a little bag in her hand.

7. Running behind her was a grey-coated man with a black moustache.

8. His hand was thrust in his pocket, and in the pocket he clutched a cobbler's awl.

9. Ahead the by-street cut into another, at right angles. There, outlined against a white wall, was a black cab-horse shaking its head, its driver hunched in sleep.

10. The old woman and the young man with the black moustache walked past some lighted windows. You could see through one window, if you looked in, an amateur mechanic sitting at a table, taking a wall-clock to pieces.

11. The mechanic had dismantled it all quite properly but could not put it back together again. He sat and scratched his head.

1. A baggage-wagon inscribed "Removals" stood at the entrance. Next to the wagon a man in a military cap explained to the yard-man who had rushed up that he was their new tenant.

2. A moment later the removal man together with the yard-man lugged a whole ton of stuff from the wagon and began to heave it up on his back to the second floor.

3. And the man in the military cap kept an anxious eye on the safety of the loads being heaved about. He had rented the flat of the mad philosopher.


1. It became even darker. The infinite expanse of roofs grew cold.

2. The roofs of many buildings merged. Some approached others and stopped where the others began.

3. Two tom cats, one black, one white, fought near a chimney flue. They both threshed about, crashing against the corrugated iron, mauling each other around the cheeks and yowling for all they were worth.

4. Humankind followed the duel with bated breath.

5. The chimney was smoking. Standing by the chimney you could see Dormidon Ivanovich's window in the distance.


1. Dormidon Ivanovich was very fond of children. He would always give them peppermint cakes, although Dormidon Ivanovich's salary was not substantial and Dormidon Ivanovich liked to eat peppermint cakes himself.

2. But he would conceal his passion.

3. Today his nephew Grisha had come to visit him. Dormidon Ivanovich gave Grisha tea to drink and peppermint cakes.

4. Grisha demolished all the cakes, not even leaving a single one for his portly uncle. Grisha showed no respect for his portly uncle and threw a rubber ball at him.

5. And Dormidon Ivanovich watched the flying ball with one eye and with the other followed the flickering lights in the philosopher's former flat.

6. Suddenly he said: "Well, there you are! People are moving in," and he gave a sigh of relief.

1. At that moment a carriage drove up to the decadent house. The fairy-tale stepped out of it together with her sister, the demi-fairy-tale.

2. Both wore Parisian spring attire and enormous black feathers fluttered on their tiny hats.

3. The fairy-tale did not know of the democrat's death. In the entrance hall they chatted together, discussing Countess Kayeva's dress.

4. At that moment in the Novodevichy Convent a fervent nun was lighting icon-lamps over certain graves, and over others she was not lighting any.

5. The fresh grave of the democrat was adorned with flowers, and a metal wreath swayed on its cross.

6. If you bent down, you could discern the meaningful inscription on the cross: "Pavel Yakovlevich Kryuchkov, born 1875, deceased 1901".

7. But the fairy-tale was unaware of the dreamer's decease and continued to chat to the demi-fairy-tale about Countess Kayeva's dress.

8. And clean-shaven people stood around them, and their faces expressed no astonishment because they knew everything and could answer everything.

9. They were . . . boors . . .

1. At that moment the young man stabbed his cobbler's awl in the old alms-woman's back and vanished into the neighbouring by-street.

2. He was a madman and police had been searching for him in vain.

3. At that moment the Cathedral of the Saviour towered over dusty Moscow liked a sacred giant.

4. Beneath the outline of its golden cupolas the waters of the Moscow River flowed on to the Caspian Sea.

1. At the very moment when the demi-fairy-tale said goodbye to the fairy-tale and the grey cat defeated the black one and the white one:

2. When the careless Grisha's ball shattered Dormidon Ivanovich's glass, and the old woman mumbled "Help" in the lonely by-street:

3. A dinner was being given by the scientists and doctors of Moscow in honour of Max Nordau. Max Nordau had blustered through the day, castigating degeneration. And now he sat in the Hermitage restaurant, all red with the excitement and the champagne.

4. He was fraternising with the scientists of Moscow.

5. A worker rolled an empty barrel past the Hermitage. It rumbled as it bounced over the roadway.

6. The point was that Moscow had no need of Nordau. It had its own life to lead. The gathering of scientists and doctors did not touch its heartstrings.

7. Here was Nordau denouncing degeneration today, and tomorrow would appear a little book by Valery Bryusov and Konstantin Bal'mont.[8]


1. Sitting at his samovar in his lonely flat on the second floor was a middle-aged man. His clear eyes looked quietly and calmly at the open door of the balcony.

2. A fresh breeze rushed in from the balcony and blew the samovar's steam into the face of the seated man.

3. He was neither old, nor young, but *passive and knowing.*

4. He was finishing his second cup of tea, and already the diamonds of the stars had dropped into the deep-blue sky.

5. He seemed to be transfixed and sat without desire, shrouded in an aimless tenderness.

6. Sirius the mystic was burning with love.

7. In black, fathomless space he belched out pillars of flame and delirium. And not just Sirius, but all the stars disgorged streams of fire into black coldness.

8. This was astral horror.

1. The *calm* and *knowing* one was not afraid of this, but went on drinking his second cup of tea.

2. It seemed he was transfixed and sat without desire, shrouded in an aimless tenderness.

3. He seemed to say: "Yes, Lord! Yes! I *know* Thee!"

4. He had already finished his second cup and was pouring himself a third.

5. And when it struck twelve in the neighbouring flat, he still sat quiet and thoughtful, his gentle gaze fixed on the moonless sky, filled with constellations.

6. It was silent. Sometimes a cab rumbled. The cats howled on the rooftops.

7. Anyone sharp of hearing would have been able to hear the summoning call of a horn in the distance.

8. As if someone stood grey-cloaked on a chimney, blowing a horn.

9. But it only appeared that way.


1. A heavy, interplanetary sphere arrived from heaven knows where.

2. With a hiss it tore into the Earth's atmosphere and, as it started glowing, emitted showers of sparks.

3. Down below it seemed as if a large glittering star had tumbled out of the deep-blue sky.

4. A white streak remained in the sky and quickly faded in the cold.

5. He saw it, he saw the star, the person sitting at the samovar, and took note of it.


1. Things happened now in the night over Moscow, full of sacred meaning.

2. Smoky blue masses would pass, to shroud the horizon now and again.

3. This was not by chance. The sacred meaning of Russia was in question.

4. The evening water barrels trundled by and answered in the negative. Some insolent people were sitting in the driver's seat and arguing with a policeman.

5. Popovsky walked by and answered in the negative.

6. But the one who sat drinking tea gave a positive answer, and Popovsky was removed from the streets of the city of Moscow: the door slammed shut behind him.


1. Max Nordau displayed great interest in the amusements the city had to offer. He was a lively, sociable man.

2. Here he was, rushing along in a Russian troika, off to the merry Mauritania restaurant, shepherded by Russian scientists.

3. He was hiccuping after the copious dinner, humming a jolly music-hall song.


1. At that time the cynical mystic from the city of Saint Petersburg shouted out to the whole of Russia, and his companions illuminated the shouter with Bengal lights.[9]

2. Even the Marxists were drawn to philosophy, and philosophers to theology.

3. But none of them knew the significance of the mysterious twinkling which was growing and growing in Russia.

4. This twinkling was reflected in Popovsky's friends who gathered in fervid Maytime meetings.

5. Each skimmed the Gospels, read the mystic and knew Dostoyevsky by heart.

6. Some went as far as to treat the late writer with intimacy.

7. Now and then you would see an eccentric tap his fingers on *The Brothers Karamazov* and throw out such words as: "Fyodor Mikhaylovich set us a riddle and now we are trying to solve it."

8. All were really such jokers that Heaven forbid you should ever meet them.


1. The spring was unprecedented and strange. Later, when summer had passed, everyone without exception remembered the spring: liberals, conservatives, mystics and realists.

2. That year there was an unheard of influx of pilgrims in Kiev. In May the forests of Ufa caught fire.

3. The inhabitants of the White Sea coast put it about that more than once a whale had swum right up to the coast of Murman and winked with its tiny fish eyes.

4. Once the inquisitive whale inquired of a deaf old coastal native: "Excuse me, old chap, but how's Ryurik keeping?"

5. And astonished the deaf old man by adding: "About a thousand years ago I swam up to this shore; Ryurik was your ruler then."


1. In the night the sound of the horn rang out especially clearly over slumbering Moscow.

2. At the same moment the officers of the crime detection department caught the crafty assailant who stabbed old women.

3. He brashly snapped his fingers at the crime detection officers and declaimed: "There are many of us in Russia."

4. And then, as though confirming his mad words, it happened that the basement rooms of the Rastorguyevs' house on Solyanka Street began to flood with sewage.

5. The city engineer already stood at the site of the crisis, arms waving, explaining to onlookers that the pipes were blocked with dirt.

6. Next day a piece appeared in the newspapers: "Sewage scandal".*


1. Six hundred old women were in a state of agitation. In the wards and corridors disgruntled senile mumblings could be heard.

* See the Moscow newspapers for May. (Author's footnote)

2. Wicked people had inflicted a wound on one of the old women by thrusting a cobbler's awl in her back.

3. The old woman sat there all bandaged up, brewing herself some camomile tea.

4. They were talking of the end of time. They seemed to see in the appearance of the assailant an omen of the Antichrist.

5. An old man was already entering the old women's section. The alms-house was mixed, for both old men and women, and six hundred old men had delegated the one to read a message of condolence to their wounded female comrade.

6. There he stood, message in hand, trying to read it. No-one understood a word. A toothless muttering was heard.


1. The brown-cassocked arch-priest sat at the samovar, chatting to a guest and wiping away the sweat standing out on his flushed forehead.

2. His guest was a learned philologist, a lecturer at Moscow University.

3. He was lean and desiccated, continually wiping his hands with a handkerchief and showering the arch-priest with quotations from the Gospel of St. John.

4. He relished every text as he revealed its sacred meaning.

5. And the arch-priest responded to his fountain of eloquence by patiently saying nothing as he chewed at the lumps of sugar and licked his lips.

6. At last he finished his glass of tea, turned it upside down as a sign he had finished his drinking and said to his guest: "What a crafty fellow you are. Ha, ha! What a crafty fellow!"

7. He turned his fleshy, purple face towards the scholar, spread his hands and, slapping himself on the stomach, added in an edifying voice: "Carry on the good work, brother scholar!"

1. An acquaintance of Popovsky's held regular literary soirées at his house, where a whole galaxy of nodding and winking intellects would forgather.

2. These soirées would be attended only by those who were able to say something new and original.

3. Nowadays the fashion was for mysticism, and so Orthodox clergy had begun to appear there.

4. Although the literary soirée host preferred sectarians, finding them more interesting.

5. As well as Kant, Plato and Schopenhauer, all those who gathered at this house had read Solov'yov,[10] were flirting with Nietzsche and attributed great significance to Hindu philosophy.

6. They had all graduated from at least two faculties and were surprised at nothing in the world.

7. Surprise they considered the most shameful weakness, and the more improbable the paper, the more credence it was granted by this group.

8. They were all people of the highest, *"many-stringed"* culture.


1. To this very place Popovsky was walking one fine spring evening.

2. He walked along beneath a fence. Clusters of white lilac spilt over the fence, waving at tiny Popovsky, but Popovsky saw nothing and smiled at a droll conjunction of thoughts.


1. As Popovsky vanished into the next by-street, Leavenovsky was walking along the same route.

2. He saw the white clusters of sweet-smelling lilac and the tender light azure of the sky.

3. He also saw a tiny star twinkling from under a branch of white lilac. He saw, too, a little cloud veiled in purple mystery.

4. All this Leavenovsky saw as he hurried towards Ostozhenka Street.

1. The contented host was wiping his white hands as he enquired whether all was in order and if there were any factors which might impede total literary fulfilment.

2. The point was that today Leavonovsky himself, a fashionable, rising talent, had promised to deliver a paper.

3. It was this that was in the solicitous host's mind, and guests were already pouring in from the diverse by-streets of Moscow.

4. Popovsky was still mincing down the same street, and behind him scurried Leavenovsky himself, still thinking of white lilac.

5. The sunset was filled with sorrow. Rosy fingers shone on turquoise enamel, as if someone quite white-haired, completely cloaked in purple raiment, were stretching his arms in benediction over the city.

6. As if someone had shaken incense. And the smoke from the incense was now melting away in a bluish flaming cloud.

7. The bells were ringing for church.


1. In Savost'yanov's bakery white loaves were rising.

2. One fat baker enquired whether there was enough leaven, and when he discovered that there was, he lit the icon-lamp.

3. Walking down the streets you could see little red or green lights in some of the windows.

4. These were icon-lamps flickering.

5. Tomorrow was Whit Sunday and the Orthodox were pouring oil into the lamps.

6. And now sacred tongues of flame burned timidly before God.

7. More than one atheist complained of stomach-ache.


1. The guests were already gathering. The contented host gave orders for tea to be served.

2. Hats and caps of diverse kinds lay in the illuminated entrance hall.

3. But the doorbell rang. Popovsky entered.

4. He removed his galoshes and headed into the hall.

5. No sooner had Popovsky arrived than Leavenovsky himself was already ringing the bell. Looking at his watch and wiping clean his pince-nez, he entered, to be hailed with greetings.

6. He offered his gracious hand to everyone. A flock of admirers already clustered about him. Nietzsche-worshippers, mystics and orgiasts converged.

7. Only one person did not come up, but stood by the window, lighting a *papirosa*.

8. He was tall and fair with black eyes. He had the face of an ascetic.

9. His short, golden beard was carefully clipped, and a flush suffused his sunken cheeks.


1. An ailing priest was here, too, in a grey cassock and wearing a golden cross.

2. His satiny hair, as white as snow, was carefully combed. He smoothed his white beard.

3. He listened more than he spoke, but his clever, deep-blue eyes looked around at those who were present . . . And each respected inwardly the old man's silence.


1. They had not yet begun the general discussion, but already the streets were becoming deserted and street-lamps were being lit one by one.

2. The sunset was attempting to pierce through a heavy cloud, which glinted in the places where it penetrated. The afterglow lasted all night at this season in Moscow, like news of a better time to come.

3. Whit Sunday, tomorrow, was glorified by the beautiful sunset searing through the smoky cloud, sending its pink benediction down to righteous and sinful alike.


1. A breeze blew in through an open window, bearing the smell of white lilac.

2. Leavenovsky still thought of white lilac, as of the oblivion of suffering and sorrows.

3. His speech began amidst the deathly attention of the audience.

4. He began to speak in a halting voice, with frequent stops to help round off his sentences.

5. After that he stopped very rarely, and phrases flew from his lips as if chiselled from ivory.

6. The old priest in the grey cassock was silent, his snow-white head bent forward, his forehead and eyes hidden by his hand.

7. The reddish light from a lamp fell upon him. The black shadow of his hand shaded his pale forehead.

8. People were sprawled on chairs, and the host tip-toed round to each of them offering tea.

9. An admirer of the Petersburg mystic sat there, picking at his pimply face.

10. Popovsky had taken refuge by the stove and had curled his lip in good time for the beginning of the paper.

11. A breeze blew in through an open window, bearing with it the smell of white lilac.

12. Leavenovsky still thought of the white lilac. He spoke of the oblivion of suffering and sorrows.


1. An enormous deep-blue cupola blotted out the sunset, its edges gleaming and glowing red. Its shadow fell over Moscow.

2. And Leavenovsky referred to the flow of time, and his eyes appeared to see misty Eternity.

3. He resurrected vanished giants; he joined their thoughts together; he could see the movement of their thought, pointing out its twists and turns.

4. And it seemed to everyone that they sat in a frail vessel amid the roar of leaden waves, and Leavenovsky was their skilled helmsman.

5. He spoke of rocket salvoes and fireworks of thoughts and dreams, asking only: *"Where are these rockets now?"*

6. He compared the thoughts of philosophers and poets with the vanished foam of an emerald sea; he asked his audience: "Where is it now?"

7. And the priest in the grey cassock was silent, his white head bent forward, his pale forehead and bright eyes hidden by his trembling hand.


1. Lightning flashed from the deep-blue cupola which had blotted out the sunset. Shadows fell on the faces of the listeners, transforming them, darkening the creases of sorrow and melancholy.

2. But it only appeared this way because of the falling shadows; and in fact their faces expressed nothing. All were satisfied with themselves and Leavenovsky.

3. Although Leavenovsky himself was satisfied neither with himself nor with the intellectual movement of the nineteenth century.

4. He compared it to the flickering of marsh fires: and asked, thumping the table: "Where are they now?"

5. And the white lilac nodded to him from the window with a greeting familiar to his heart: the oblivion of flowers.

6. The blue cupola slipped away from the sunset. The sunset laughed from under the cupola with heartfelt, childish laughter.

7. Leavenovsky thumped the table, and in Leavenovsky's eyes the pink sunset was reflected . . . And Leavenovsky seemed an overgrown, good-natured child.


1. A period of sorrow. He stood among the audience, pulling his black moustache, nodding his head derisively.

2. He was burying philosophy, and cried and sobbed over its burial mound like the Old Testament Jeremiah.

3. A period of anger. He stood among the audience in deathly silence. He silently threatened the positivists.

4. He roared that they had removed the colours from heaven.

5. Then he began to laugh demonically as he spoke of democrats, populists and Marxists.

6. But a breeze must have blown from the deceased democrat's grave, because someone whispered to Leavenovsky: "Do not disturb my rest", and the ivory phrases ceased to fly from his ardent lips.

7. The priest in the grey cassock, too, was silent, his white head bent forward, his pale forehead and deep-blue eyes hidden by his trembling hand.

8. On the floor lay his black shadow.


1. And for a long time, for such a long time, Leavenovsky was silent and looked like an overgrown, good-natured child, the wind stirring his black hair, and his grey eyes fixed upon the window.

2. And an unconscious tenderness softened Leavenovsky's features, as if he were preparing to utter a new truth.

3. At that moment in the Cathedral of the Assumption they were singing *Hail, gladdening light* and the bishops' mitres were shining.

4. The smoke from the incense rose up to the cupola of the Cathedral.


1. And then everyone suddenly sensed the shrill murmur of melting glaciers, and Leavenovsky opened his mouth again with the prophetic word: *Superman.*

2. The Nietzsche-worshippers began to move their chairs, and the old priest raised his bright eyes towards Leavenovsky,

3. Whose words flashed with a trembling flame, and in the room there started up a whirlwind of fire and light.

4. As if they could feel the proximity of melting snow, as if a delirious man had been given a cooling drink.

5. As if the heat-induced horror were sinking in a damp, misty marsh, and Leavenovsky pointed to the sacred significance of Superman.

6. He studded his speech with pearls of Holy Scripture as he descended to the theological depths.

7. He cited past beliefs, and compared them with today's most burning questions.

8. He expected spiritual renewal, expected the possible synthesis of theology, mysticism and the church, pointed to the three transformations of the spirit.[11]

9. He sang hymns to the child of the tribe of Juda.

10. His words flickered with a trembling flame and — fiery images — vanished through the open windows.

11. Sometimes he would stop, listening to the *Waltz of the Snowflakes* being played somewhere in the distance.

12. And then everyone could see that a lotus flower was held over Leavenovsky — tender oblivion of suffering and sorrows.

13. This was the oblivion of flowers, and from under an opal cloud the bright sunset laughed with heartfelt, childish laughter.

14. Leavenovsky thumped the table, and in Leavenovsky's eyes the pink sunset was reflected . . . And Leavenovsky looked like an overgrown, innocent child.

15. In his eyes too strong a tenderness was reflected; you could feel that a string had been pulled too tight, would break together with the dream.

16. Somewhere the *Waltz of the Snowflakes* was being played. The soul of each was whitening to the point of snow. Freezing in blissful torpor.

17. Impossible, tender, eternal, cherished, familiar and strange at all times.

18. Thus he spoke. The old priest, gripping the arm of his chair, looked into his eyes with a welcoming, tender expression.

19. All were excited and amazed.

1. The contented host held his white hands out to the paper's discomfited author. There was a lively sound of voices . . .

2. A Marxist, here by accident, leaped from his chair and thundered in to look at him and seemed to be saying: *"I know. Oh, I know."*

3. But at this point he was interrupted by a fair-haired man with a golden beard and an austere and thoughtful face. He looked like an ascetic with sunken eyes and a feverish flush.

4. During Leavenovsky's speech his good-natured eyes had been raised to look at him and seemd to be saying: *"I know. Oh, I know . . ."*

5. Now he stood like a powerful dictator. Soon his expressionless voice had silenced even the extrmely erudite.


1. He said: "The Third Kingdom is now dawning, the Kingdom of the Spirit . . . Water and pale mist are at this moment closer than sacrificial blood."

2. "Although the Kingdom of Heaven will not come by water alone, but by blood and the Spirit."

3. "Now we shall have to suffer the terrible final battle."

4. "There will be amongst us some who will fall, and some who will forbid, and some who will perceive and see and proclaim."

5. "The time of the four horsemen is dawning: the white, the red, the black and the pale rider of death."

6. "First the white, then the red, then the black and finally the pale."

7. "Do you not see that *something* is descending upon us, or rather: *Someone.*"

8. "He will be the tenderest flower amid earthly gardens, a new rung on Jacob's ladder."

9. "He will be a mountain stream springing up into everlasting life."

10. "This was the mysterious thought of Dostoyevsky. This was the heart-rending cry of Nietzsche."

11. "And the Spirit and the bride say: Come."

1. And still the old priest was silent, his head, filled with thoughts, bent forward, his face hidden by his trembling hand.

2. A shadow was cast by his hand, and the priest's deep-blue eyes looked out of the shadow.

3. In the cathedrals they were already singing the evening doxology. You could hear the tinkling of censers and the sighs of the old bishops, crowned in their diamond-studded hats.


1. The prophet was saying: "And the Spirit and the bride say: Come."

2. "I hear the thundering of a horse's hooves: it is the first rider."

3. "His horse is white. He himself is *white*: on his head is a golden crown. He has come forth to conquer."

4. "He is a man. He is to rule all nations with a rod of iron. As the vessels of a potter shall those who will not obey be broken to shivers."

5. "He is our Ivan-Tsarevich. Our *white* standard-bearer."

6. "His mother is the woman clothed with the sun. And she has been given wings so that she might flee the Serpent and escape into the wilderness."

7. "There a *white* child will grow up to shine forth at the rising of the sun."

8. "And the Spirit and the bride say: Come."


1. Then he stood, austere and thoughtful.

2. He was a fair-haired, tall man with black eyes. A flush suffused his sunken cheeks.

3. He was sunk in thoughtful silence, and the Marxist, forgetting his objections, furtively vanished from this *mad house*.

4. But a white breeze blew in through an open window; it was bringing the prophet sweet, lilac kisses. And the clear evening glow laughed and whispered: *"My dear ones."*

5. Leavenovsky fervently shook the fair-haired prophet's hand, and the

old priest looked silently around at those who were present with his deep-blue eyes and then bent his head down to his old man's chest.

6. Then he shaded himself from the light with his hand. A breeze began to flutter his satiny white hair.

7. On the floor lay his black shadow.


1. At that moment in the Arabian Desert a lion was resolutely roaring; it was from the tribe of Juda.

2. But here, too, on the roofs of Moscow the cats howled.

3. The roofs merged into each other, deserts of green above the slumbering city.

4. On the roofs you could observe a prophet.

5. He performed his nightly walk above the slumbering city, soothing fears, banishing terrors.

6. His grey eyes spat out sparks from beneath eyelashes so black they seemed to be outlined in charcoal. His greying beard fluttered in the wind.

7. It was the late Vladimir Solov'yov.

8. He wore a grey cloak and a large, wide-brimmed hat.

9. Sometimes he would remove a horn from the pocket of his cloak and blow a clarion-call across the slumbering city.

10. Many people heard the sound of the horn but did not know what it meant.

11. Solov'yov stepped bravely across the roofs. Above him diamond trails of stars were spilling out.

12. The Milky Way seemed closer than it should. Sirius the mystic was burning with love.

13. At one moment Solv'yov would appeal to slumbering Moscow with his vibrant horn, at another he would thunder out his poem:

> Evil forgotten
> Sinks in blood! . . .
> Arises cleansed
> The sun of love! . . .

14. The beautiful dawn, red and mad, laughed as she burnt through a jasper-coloured cloud.


1. In a room a reddish icon-lamp was burning. The child awoke.

2. It cried out in a clear voice: "Nanny."

3. The grumbling nanny woke up and tried to calm the boy.

4. And he stretched out his little hands towards her and said with a smile: "There's a horn blowing somewhere!"

5. The nanny made the sign of the cross over him, saying: "Christ be with you, my dear! You dreamed it!"

6. And the boy went back to sleep, smiling. And the nanny went off to bed.

7. Both of them heard the summoning horn in their sleep . . . It was Solov'yov walking the roofs of the buildings, soothing fears, banishing terrors.


1. The dawn was already aflame with new strength when the ailing priest arose from his armchair.

2. He was talking of universal love with downcast eyes.

3. A gentle breeze blew his satiny locks, and the old priest's lips broke into a sorrowful smile.

4. He did not accept or reject a word of what had been said, but he spoke of love.

5. And there was the breeze . . . And they did not know if it came from the sweet, sighing lilacs or from the white words of Father Ioann.

6. And the mad dawn set light to the jasper-coloured cloud and laughed

now as she blazed, bedecking herself with the silver morning star.

1. Father Ioann said little. Then he sat by the window on that glowing May night, his white head bent down to his chest . . .

1. In the morning Leavenovsky was on his way back from Ostozhenka Street, tired and sleepy.

2. He often yawned because it was full daylight.

3. Fragrant clusters of lilac oblivion spilt down, outlined against the turquoise sky.

4. A purple mystery was being enacted above a snow-white cloud.

5. All this Leavenovsky had seen as he hurried towards Ostozhenka Street.

1. A pilgrim walked along with a knapsack over his shoulders, his narrow, grey little beard thrust vigorously forward, radiating the joy of universal forgiveness.

2. The pine forest was already behind him. The sun stood in benediction above the green pine trees.

3. Tiny yellowish-white clouds which seemed fashioned from wax stood out in relief against the deepening blue sky.

4. And in front of him stretched the plain. Above the plain shone the gold and silver cupolas of sacred places.

5. This was Moscow lit up by the sunbeams of May. This was Moscow on Whit Sunday.

6. The grey-bearded pilgrim gazed with curosity over the sacred places to seek out Moscow's mysteries and rejoiced to himself.

7. He was shrewd and nothing amazed him. Amazement he considered *human, all too human.*

8. Tiny yellowish-white clouds which seemed fashioned from wax were scudding across the sky, and in his mind the pilgrim lit candles to the Moscow saints.

1. Father Ioann was conducting a service in his parish.

2. The bells rang welcomingly to the glory of the Holy Trinity from his clean little white church with its silver cupolas.

3. They were singing the hymn to the cherubim. Everyone was covered with sweat. An enigmatic deacon in his gleaming vestments periodically bowed, as he swung the censer.

4. Rays of gold were bursting in through the narrow windows and coming to rest on the gleaming vestments. A fine wisp of incense hung softly in the sunbeams.

5. The royal gates concealed no mysteries: Father Ioann's hands were raised in benediction, and his satiny white hair fell back from his pale forehead.

6. Then Father Ioann would bow low before the holy altar and streams of mysterious words would escape from his tightly pressed lips.

7. Thus he would be transfixed, a mysterious symbol, interrupting his prayers with a dreamy sigh.


1. Then the great entrance took place. Two children, their robes glittering, were bearing wax candles. Behind them walked the golden deacon.

2. Quietly following all of them came Father Ioann, chalice in hand. His eyes shone. His vestments gleamed. His hair flowed down in a snowy wave.

3. And the congregation bowed in the rays of the May sun.


1. And while Father Ioann conducted his service, Father Damian was doing the same thing in a neighbouring church.

2. Services were being held in all the churches; the same sacred words were being uttered, but by different voices.

3. The priests without exception were arrayed in gold brocade. Some were white-haired, others fat, others good-looking, many were ugly.

4. In the Church of the Saviour an unknown golden-mitred bishop officiated.

5. His crozier was held by a lay brother, and he himself delivered his benediction from the royal gates, crossing the *dikirion* with the *trikirion*.[12]

1. Dormidon Ivanovich stood through the service. He sweated profusely and, as he left, mopped himself with a handkerchief.

2. His fat fingers clutched a five kopeck piece of communion bread, appropriated for the well-being of God's servant Dormidon.

3. At the exit the clerk Openkin respectfully wished him the compliments of the seaon, and at home Matryona set the samovar before him.

4. Dormidon Ivanovich crossed himself devoutly and consumed on an empty stomach the piece of communion bread for the well-being of God's servant Dormidon.

5. As he brewed the tea, he said to the cook: "Well, Matryona, God has sent us his blessing!"

6. In church this portly section-head had exuded his sweat thoroughly, and now he just as thoroughly absorbed this Chinese fluid.

1. The by-street was bathed in sun. The road was turning white. In place of the sky there hung a gigantic turqoise.

2. The neo-classical house had six columns, and on the six columns stood six white, stone maidens.

3. The stone maidens had six stone cushions on their heads, and the cornice of the house rested on the cushions.

4. In the little asphalt courtyard stood a pile of damp red sand.

5. Blond-curled children played on the pile of sand dressed in sailors' jackets with red anchors.

6. They sank their little hands into the cold sand and threw the sand in handfuls over the dry asphalt.

7. On top of the pile of sand stood a little boy; his face was austere and thoughtful. His deep-blue eyes absorbed the colour of the sky. His curly hair was soft as flax and tumbled in dreamy waves onto his shoulders.

8. With austere authority the little boy held in his hands an iron piston, found heaven knows where. The child was beating his little sisters with a rod of iron, as the vessels of a potter breaking them to shivers.

9. His little sisters squealed and threw handfuls of sand at the despot.

10. With austere authority the boy wiped the red sand from his face and looked thoughtfully up at the turquoise of the sky as he leaned on his rod.

11. Then suddenly he abandoned his iron piston, leaped from the pile of sand and ran along the asphalt courtyard, crying out joyfully.

12. A cab carried Leavenovsky by. Leavenovsky was proceeding to the fair-haired prophet to talk about general mysteries.


1. A monk was walking aong a fashionable street. His head-dress rose high above his lean face.

2. He wore a silver cross and walked quickly through the festive crowd.

3. His black beard reached down to his waist; it began right beneath his eyes.

4. His eyes were sad and mournful despite the fact that it was Whitsunday.

5. Suddenly the monk stopped and spat superstitiously. A malicious smile twisted his austere features.

6. This happened because the cynical mystic had uttered yet another new thought, and it had been published in *Polar Patterns*.


1. Prophets and prelates had been on display in the window of an art shop on Kuznetsky Bridge Street.

2. And the prophets appeared to be shouting from behind the glass windows, stretching their bare hands towards the street, shaking their sorrowful heads.

3. The prelates, however, looked serene and smiled quietly, hiding a crafty grin in their whiskers.

4. People clustered by the windows with wide-open mouths.


1. Golden streams of light flooded into the windows of the decadent house.

2. They fell on a mirror. The mirror reflected the next room. From where the sound of suppressed sobbing could be heard.

3. In the middle of the flowers and silk stood the fairy-tale who had turned very pale. Her reddish hair gleamed in the gold of the sun and her pale violet dress was covered with white irises.

4. She had found out at the festival of flowers about the death of the dreamer, and now the orphaned fairy-tale was wringing her slender white hands.

5. Her coral-coloured lips trembled and silver pearls ran down her pale marble cheeks, freezing in the irises pinned to her breast.

6. She stood distraught and weeping, looking out of the window.

7. And from the window the mad dawn laughed at her tears, as it burnt through a jasper-coloured cloud.

8. The fairy-tale's tears were futile because the time of democrats was passing.

9. The wave of time had washed away the dreamer, had borne him away to eternal rest.

10. This is what the mad dawn told her, laughing to the point of exhaustion, and the fairy-tale wept over the scattered irises.

11. And . . . in the next . . . room stood the shattered centaur. He had entered this room . . . and seen the reflection of his nymph.

12. He stood there stunned, not believing the looking-glass reflection, not daring to verify the perfidous mirror.

13. Two sorrowful wrinkles creased the brow of the good-natured centaur, and he pulled pensively at his elegant beard.

14. Then he quietly left this room.

1. The fairy-tale ordered the carriage to be harnessed. She wanted to take a scarlet rose and place it on the dreamer's grave.

2. And the golden Whitsunday passed to be replaced by Whitsunday evening.

3. The memory of the dreamer was sitting in a tiny boat and floated off into the distance of an emerald sea.

4. The years were passing, bearing other tidings: something had had its day and reposed in the cemetery; something grieved in the lunatic asylum; something oppressed the fairy-tale's heart.

5. And, enveloped in the sunset, she stretched out her slender, white hands towards the evening light.

6. She seemed to be whispering: "May eternal anguish fly away into interplanetary space."

7. "And may it call back from there so that it can shine forth once more."

8. The fairy-tale stood like this for a long time, talking to the sunset, and it seemed a sacred vision.

9. The memory of the dreamer was sitting in a tiny boat and floated off into the distance of an emerald sea: it was a girl in a necklace of tears.

10. And hanging over the emerald sea was a cloud with opal edges.

11. Like a dreamy giant, it was melting away on the turquoise enamel.

12. This was the nymph's glowing farewell to the memory of the dreamer.

13. The memory gave a sorrowful smile and rowed into the uncharted distance because a different time was approaching, bearing other tidings.

 

1. The pale golden-bearded ascetic with the faint flush was giving Leavenovsky some tea.

2. Leavenovsky was splashing the tea in excitement and, gripping the ascetic by the hands and almost choking, he said: "So you know the woman clothed with the sun?"

3. But the pale ascetic said impassively: "I know nothing: all this is still very uncertain . . . The material is only being written . . . There will be no conclusions before summer . . ."

4. And from the open window the golden Whitsunday evening was asking to be let into the room.

5. The window blew steam from the samovar into Leavenovsky's face. The golden-bearded ascetic was looking at him as you would at a good-natured child.


1. On that golden Whitsunday evening a consumptive was dying. A bouquet of white lilac stood on the table in his room.

2. The blinds were down. But rays of sunshine managed to force their way through them by stealth.

3. And there was Father Ioann coming up to the house. His satiny white hair stood out clearly against the dusty roadway.

4. The door, behind which red horrors hid, gave a creak and Ioann stood on the threshold before the consumptive.

5. His deep-blue eyes were fixed on the sick man, and he made the sign of the cross over him with his trembling hand.


1. Then the sick man felt an ebbing of terror. Raising himself a little from his bed of fever, he gave his holy friend a bitter smile.

2. He compained to Ioann of the terrors which oppressed him, and the old priest raised a branch of white lilac to his face.

3. He complained of his sins, but Ioann took off his silver cross, and the cold metal scorched the feverish lips of the dying man.

4. In fear the sick man pressed himself against his holy friend, shouting out that he feared death.

5. And Ioann knelt to pray before the bed of fever. His satiny hair was white as snow, and his pale forehead shone with other-worldly meekness.

6. Then the white priest bent down joyfully over the dying man and sə with a smile that the Lord was summoning him.

1. The priest opened the window. The golden evening fell on the sick man.

2. And the sick man died, on that golden Whitsunday evening. His holy friend kissed him for the last time, after adorning the bed with white lilac.

3. Soon the servants bustled in alarm around their dead master, but Father Ioann was walking back along the dusty streets.

4. The gentle bells of the little silver church summoned him to celebrate the all-night vigil.


1. The vigil had not yet begun, but the crimson icon-lamps were already burning.

2. The royal gates were closed and draped with red silk within.

3. But the meek Father Ioann passed by, bowing low to the devout.

4. He had just sent his rich parishioner to the next world: the one who had been afraid to depart on such a distant journey. Ioann had equipped him carefully.

5. And in the sky a cumulus giant swirled smokily, with opal-coloured edges.

6. The giant was burning with tenderness in the cold of the pure turquoise.

7. This conflagration contained both the love of the old Ioann and the love of the fairy-tale for the memory of the dreamer.

8. And the memory floated off into the distance of an emerald sea: it was a young girl in a necklace of tears.


1. Within the cloister the pink cathedral with its gold and white cupolas rose into the sky. All around it were marble tombstones and wrought iron shrines.

2. The trees murmured over the lonely dead.

3. This was the kingdom of frozen tears.

4. Near a little red cottage a nun sat beneath an apple tree, sprinkled with white flowers.

5. Her eyes were other-worldly and lost in contemplation of the sunset; a rosy flush played on her young cheeks.

6. Her black head-dress rose above her marble forehead. And she fingered her rosary convulsively.

7. She had fallen in love with the beautiful sunset. It laughed into her face, lighting up both the nun and the red cottage.

8. And the austere Mother Superior protruded her head from the cottage and looked at the nun suspiciously.

9. The rasping screech of stone-martins could be heard, while the nun was aimlessly burning in the glow of the sunset.

10. Her gentle hands fingered a black rosary. She had raised her shoulders high and was transfixed beneath the snowy apple tree.

11. Here and there on the graves little flames were sending out puffs of smoke.

12. The black nun would light icon lamps over certain graves and over others she would not light any.

13. The wind rattled the metal wreaths, and a clock was striking the hour.

14. The dew was falling on a grey stone shrine engraved with the words: "Peace be with you, Anna, my wife."


1. Suddenly the nun heard the rustle of a silk dress and awoke from the aimless tenderness.

2. A beautiful young woman was walking before her, with sad, deep-blue eyes and wearing pale-violet Parisian clothes.

3. Her red hair flamed in the burning glow of the sunset, and her horses snorted, waiting at the gates of the cloister for their mistress to return . . .

4. Their clear eyes met: both had blue, blue eyes.

5. Both were like nymphs: one dressed in black, and the other in pale-violet; one pressed a perfumed handkerchief to her face, the other convulsively fingered a rosary, and the black head-dress swayed above her little marble face.

6. They understood each other; they shared the same sorrow.

7. And through the rustling trees black swallows screeched and the mischievous sunset peeped out at them.

8. The sunset gave a good-natured laugh and blew a breeze to the snowy apple tree. And the apple tree sprinkled the black nun with fragrant white flowers.


1. And already it was night. The nuns, with downcast eyes, dispersed to their own cells. The lights were being snuffed out at their little windows.

2. That same thing arose, eternally cherished and pensively sad.

3. The wreaths swayed. As if the deceased were walking about adjusting the wicks in the icon-lamps; they were kissing the freshly brought flowers with their bloodless lips.

4. But this was not happening.

5. And only the silver angel continued to stand above the tiny shrine in frozen prayer, and the clock struck the hours monotonously.

6. Time flew over the peaceful cloister as a breath of wind, bending the young birch trees. And conversing with it was the other-worldly woman in black.

7. Her pale face was frozen with eternal sorrow and deprivation, and reflected in her grey eyes was misty Eternity.

8. Thus she stood among the dewy graves, with flames flickering here and there, and she whispered scarcely audibly: *"Here it is, Lord, the one thing, eternally one and the same! . . ."*

9. Rattling the metal wreaths, the wind spread her other-worldly, sacred sorrow far and wide.

10. The dark-blue outline of the old grey stone shrine stood out amongst the graves, and the dew already covered the stone words: "Peace be

with you, Anna, my wife!" . . .

1. It was a holy night. The last little cloud melted away in the enamel sky.

2. The enamel sky burnt with golden stars; the streets were empty, clean and white.

3. If you went out onto the balcony of a three-storeyed house, you could see two lines of golden lamp lights along the sleeping streets.

4. In the distance the lights merged into one single, golden thread.

1. The horizon did not die down at all that night, but shone. As if a sacred candle were flaming beyond the horizon.

2. As if, beyond the horizon, St. John the Divine had prayed all night, enacting a purple mystery.

3. A long, narrow, amber cloud stood on the horizon.

4. Grieving, the fairy-tale sat on a high window ledge. She was looking at the amber cloud.

5. Her reddish hair had fallen about her shoulders, and the golden stars shone into her face.

6. Tomorrow she would leave Moscow and say farewell to her dreams.

7. . . . As if a sacred candle were flaming beyond the horizon.

8. As if, beyond the horizon, St. John the Divine had prayed all night, enacting a purple mystery.

1. A white Whit Monday had already dawned. All were resting in bright dreams.

2. Only on the balcony of a three-storeyed house did a person appear, neither young, nor old.

3. He held a candle in his hand. The candle flamed on that white Whit Monday.

4. A strong wind had blown up, although the sky was boundless and clear.

5. The grey dust rose in long, swirling columns.

6. The chimneys sang and groaned, and the candle held by the man on the balcony went out.

7. The clear sound of a horn drifted over Moscow, and whirlwinds of light swept down from above, streams of light on that white Whit Monday.

## PART THREE

1. The wind breathed coolness. The emerald cornfields were bent in prayer to the azure morning.

2. In the distance ploughed fields stood out blackly.

3. A horse would appear here and there and behind it a peasant dragging a plough, carving the earth into deep furrows.

4. The peasants and horses were different, but what they did was the same.

5. The ordinary eye would see nothing unusual here, though a careful observer would reason otherwise.


1. Travelling down the dusty road amid the pale green cornfields came a troika. The driver dressed in a sleeveless velvet jacket urged the tired horses on.

2. Seated in the troika was a fair-haired gentleman wearing a city coat. He was piled round with suitcases.

3. The cool air had misted the lenses of his pince-nez; and so he had removed it to wipe them, squinting from side to side with his black, shortsighted eyes and singing softly: "Black earth country's meadows, fields of gold and emerald . . . Never stinting, tireless, patient earth . . ."

4. This was a poem by Vladimir Solov'yov, and the person seated in the troika was an admirer of the deceased philosopher.

5. So here was the golden-bearded ascetic travelling along to his brother's estate to rest after the winter's hurly-burly.

6. Here he was squinting all about himself and at the cornfields with his short-sighted black eyes and whispering: "Emerald fields . . . Vladimir Sergeyevich had a marvellous way of putting it . . . They are indeed quite emerald! . . .„

7. But his wonder was not shared by the driver in the sleeveless velvet jacket; he was clicking his tongue and urging the horses on.


1. From time to time they would pass ploughed fields. Here and there a horse would appear, and behind it a peasant dragging a plough, carving the earth into deep furrows.

2. The peasants and horses were different, but what they did was the same.

3. Here was an old giant of a man — a stooping rural Hercules — trampling the freshly turned earth with his bast shoes, as he hurried after the plough.

4. There was a puny little peasant doing the same thing, shaking his wisp of a beard.

5. The peasants and horses were different, but what they did was the same.


1. Sometimes the plain would be cut by deep ravines, and would shape itself into a high plateau.

2. There was something Buddhist in this alternation of plain and ravine.

3. It brought the past to mind more than the present. The Mongol past.

4. At least this was the thought of the golden-bearded ascetic, as he sat in state amid his suitcases.

5. He whispered to himself: "Here is your Russian sorrow and Russian aimlessness . . ."

6. And from above the sun had already begun to burn the back of his neck for this audacious thought.

1. He could see the majestic debris of the past, and from the past the future ascended, wreathed in shrouds of smoke.

2. He considered that the culmination of the synthetic era in any culture demanded a great personality; only the hand of a great teacher could bind the final knots and unite the coloured ribbons of events.

3. He thought that the light had ceased to shine in the west and that the black wings of night approached across the misty ocean.

4. European culture had uttered its word . . . And this word had arisen like an ominous symbol . . . And this symbol was a dancing skeleton . . .

5. And skeletons had begun to run the length of senescent Europe, their gloomy eye-sockets flickering.

6. This is what he thought as he received a jolt: the road was a mass of pot-holes, and the golden-bearded ascetic said to himself: "Patience."

7. "Patience", because in the east hot blood still rippled in the golden chalices, and around the chalices stood hierophants, and a dark blue fragrance was soaring to heaven to the sound of tinkling censers.

8. He dreamt of uniting the western skeleton with eastern blood. He wished to clothe this skeleton with flesh.

9. Sitting amid suitcases, he divined Russia's part in this grand union, and the driver, turning his dusty face towards him, said with a smile: "You'll not be used to our roads, sir."

10. But the golden-bearded ascetic made an effort to smile, as he looked around at the hopelessness of the plains.

11. He asked if they had much further to go till they reached the Gryazishchi Estate, and having learnt that Gryazishchi was still a long way off, he broke loose from the suitcases and soared away on the wings of fantasy.


1. The sun was becoming merciless, brimming with scorching cruelty. In the distance gleamed the cross of a white church.

2. Where the humpbacked plain cut off the horizon a lonely group of people could be seen heading eastwards.

3. They carried two red and gold gonfalons which fluttered on their tall poles.

4. The peasant women wore red headbands, and gold ribbons glinted on their deep-blue skirts. They carried a representation of the Byzantine saints.

5. They walked with their icons and gonfalons to the next estate to pray for rain.

6. They walked in a lonely group with banners spread wide.

7. This was a call to the prophet Elijah. A sacred appeal for drenching rain and shafts of fire.

8. This was a challenge to the noontide loss of faith.

9. Soon the tiny group of banner-bearers vanished into the endless plain and in the distance gleamed the cross of a white church.


1. The ascetic was already approaching his beloved Gryazischi, as he counted his followers on his fingers.

2. He zealously breathed sorrow for whirlwinds of fire into their hearts so that they should be kindled by this sorrow and be consumed by love.

3. Sacred days were approaching and summoning the prophets . . . And the prophets slumbered in people's hearts.

4. He wanted to wake them from their slumbers and summon them to the golden morning.

5. He saw mankind as having paused in some kind of somnolent meditation.

6. The pastured sheep had wandered off in all directions in search of some new truth, yet to be found. This was the noontide dream amid the drought of summer.

7. And the best in mankind which was not yet asleep was turning into sectarian madness and the ecstasy of delirium.

8. Oh yes, he knew something, he certainly knew something, the golden-bearded ascetic! So here he was, travelling into the country to rest after the winter's hurly-burly.

9. He needed to crown the walls which he had erected with a cupola — to draw his own conclusions from the material he had accumulated.

10. He wanted to give a blazing sermon to his pupils in Moscow. They were lively people who had grasped the wisdom of science and philosophy. Morning stars, like Leavenovsky, flickered there.

11. Leavened pastry, placed in the oven by a skilful baker.

12. Many of them were already rubbing reality from their eyes to lose themselves in dreams with a pure heart.

13. Soon a cascade of diamonds would shower his impoverished country. Soon the stars of prophecies would descend from the skies.

14. The vault of heaven seemed to be painted on porcelain.

15. On the horizon whirlwind columns of black dust were rising.

16. A black funnel rose and then, breaking up, scattered away the dust into the indifferent heavens.


1. He had *seen*, he had *seen*, the golden-bearded ascetic, and he *knew* something! . . .

2. He had seen the titans of destruction, overgrown with thoughts like furry animals covered with hair, burying Europe one cloudy autumn day.

3. It was drizzling and the wind moaned despondently, drowning out the tears of the poor mothers.

4. They walked behind the black coffin dressed in clothes resembling the night with a picture of a skull on their gloomy cowls and with torches of horror in their hands.

5. They carried cushions with silver tassels, and lying on the cushions were the horrific regalia.

6. Behind the coffin were the leading and most horrific gravediggers.

7. The Norwegian lion was there, whose roaring had irritated the deceased,[13] and thick-skinned Silas Singlewit held a splinter of wood in one hand and an axe in the other.[14] He was planing the splinter and droning: "The peasant way, the stupid way! Sing sheep, pig and goat!

Any which and ever way, and out comes a boat!"

8. And Zarathustra — the black, ravening panther who had finished Europe off.

9. The Belgian recluse was there as well,[15] and the French monk dressed as a bat and holding a magical censer in his hand.

10. Sitting on his shoulder was a black cat, licking its paw and urging guests to come to the funeral.[16]

11. The singer of falsehood was there, too, vegetating in a dungeon,[17] and the Parisian magus.[18]

12. And the Milanese,[19] and Max — the curly-headed poodle, yelping about degeneration, and John Ruskin who confused the concepts of good, truth and beauty — as he stirred the sugary gruel of contemporary life.

13. And the misplaced caricature of the Christian superman whose name is *super-impotence*, borne aloft by the Vatican guard on a rotting litter and wearing a paper nightcap.

14. This was a clockwork doll meant to parody Christianity.

15. Barren thistle, sprung from a roadside boulder! Roman parasite! Holiness, lit up by electricity![20]

16. Trudging behind the great gravediggers came the hordes of lesser ones. They triumphed not through quality, but quantity.

17. Gnomes who had slipped into childhood; lisping old men not three feet high.

18. They carried little green lamps wrapped round with crape, and on the funereal ribbons you could read: *"nervous disorder"*, *"debauchery"*, *"indifference"*, *"feeblemindedness"*, *"mania"*.

19. But the most dangerous mania was the mania of false erudition. This consisted of a person clawing his eyes out and with his arrogant fingers forcing convexo-convex lenses into his bleeding eye-sockets.

20. The world would look different: an inverted, reduced image.

21. This was a horror and was known as exact science.

22. Future destroyers were there as well, indescribable in their horror.

23. The eyes of all were fixed on the black veil of night which had spread soundlessly over the Northern sea, the German sea.

24. It seemed to be an enormous bat which had blotted out the sun.

25. The leaden waves ran up to the sandy shore and hurled forth a beast with seven heads and ten horns.

26. And the teachers of abomination great and small cried out: "Who is like unto the beast?"

27. Illuminated by gas-jets the beast approached dead Europe, and she opened her dead eyes and began to mumble with her toothless mouth.

28. And she painted herself and simpered before the beast, and her words were more than ominous, and she opened her dead eyes and began to mumble with her toothless mouth.

29. And then each of the great gravediggers and great blackguards (as the teachers of abomination were called) adorned her nocturnal crown with his own false jewel.

30. Here was Zarathustra's red ruby and Huysmans' black diamond.

31. John Ruskin's Carrara marble and the cobble-stone of Russia's Singlewit.

32. But all of these were imitation jewels; they flickered with a strange light above the wig of the great whore.

33. But all of these were imitation jewels; the moon was crimson, and all felt a surge of inexplicable horror.

34. And they said to the mountains: "Fall down upon us!" But the mountains did not fall. And there was no hiding their faces from the horror.

35. And they were filled with horror to the very last one.


1. And while he was thinking these thoughts, prayers for rain were being said on the neighbouring estate.

2. Amidst the emerald cornfields turning to yellow, red and gold gonfalons fluttered like sacred invocatory banners.

3. The priest placed birch twigs in a vessel filled with water and sprinkled it over the cornfields, praying for a *seasonable change of weather*.

4. A lone peasant, barefoot and dirty, vanished away somewhere amid the cornfields.

5. And only the sound of his anguished voice spread over the fields.


1. The ascetic continued his fantasy. To spite the black wings of night he tripled the brightness of the light in the north-east.

2. The orb of Sunday was already rising in the sky, its sacred flame banishing the horror of plague from the east.

3. In the east people were not filled with terror. Joyful excitement had long been obvious here, as if the seraphim had stirred up an invisible agitation.

4. And when the beast ascended the throne with the great whore, the flames of prophets appeared over Holy Russia.

5. Her apostle was John whose gaze had penetrated into the depths of the final centuries.

6. Then there appeared a sign before the faces of those who waited: the woman clothed with the sun was moving on the two wings of an eagle towards the Solovetsky monastery,

7. To be delivered there of a man child who was to rule all nations with a rod of iron.

8. There came to pass the ancient prophecy of the white rider who was to go forth conquering.

9. And there was a great battle between the warriors of the beast and of the woman. And when the battle reached the climax, an angel was seen ascending in the east.

10. He stood between the Tigris and the Euphrates. He poured out the vessel of God's wrath onto the west, crying out: "Babylon is fallen, is fallen, that great city!"

11. And he destroyed the whore and the beast and bound the devil for a thousand years.

12. This was the first resurrection — like unto the second, and this was the first death — like unto the second.

13. This was the sign divined by the prophets.

14. He had *seen*, he had *seen*, the golden-bearded ascetic, and he *knew* something!


1. He whispered entreatingly: "Woman clothed with the sun, reveal thyself to thy standard-bearer! Hear thy prophet!"

2. And suddenly his awesome expression showed great confusion.

3. He remembered a familiar image: two deep-blue eyes framed by reddish hair, a silvery voice and the sorrow of other-worldly lips.

4. With one fluttering hand she had been cooling herself with a fan, responding to vacuous remarks with vacuous remarks.

5. He had seen her like this at the ball given by the Marshal of Nobility.

6. He whispered in confusion: "The woman clothed with the sun," and already the troika approached the entrance.

7. Standing on the hop-twined steps was the golden-bearded ascetic's brother, landowner Pavel Musatov with herculean shoulders and a large beard.

8. His frog-eyed face laughed and beamed, framed by a fair-haired beard as soft as flax . . . Smoke rose from a cigar in his left hand.

9. The wind was blowing his tight-fitting coat of white tussore, and he was waving to his brother with a handkerchief.


1. Standing in the cool hallway was his niece Varya who was staying at her uncle's house with her consumptive mother.

2. She was a pallid blonde girl with dreamy eyes, a tiny nose and freckles.

3. The Musatov brothers embraced and kissed each other.

1. A lone peasant, barefoot and dirty, vanished away somewhere amid the cornfields.

2. And only the sound of his anguished voice spread over the wide steppes.


1. In the dining-room luncheon was set. Here Pavel Musatov joyfully downed six glasses of cherry brandy.

2. Then he grabbed hold of his laughing niece and danced a mazurka with her.

3. He danced up and down in front of his brother in a sprightly way, stamping his glossy boots.

4. He was a retired guards' officer.

5. The girl was laughing and so was he, while his stomach and watch-chain ornaments shook, and beads of sweat appeared on his face which had turned purple.

6. He was full of wonder, the golden-bearded ascetic, who had arrived in the country to draw his conclusions about the fate of the world from the material he had accumulated.

7. But everyone was happy.

8. Brother Pavel had already unbuttoned his tussore coat and was wiping his frog-eyed face with a handkerchief.


1. At luncheon, while cleaning a fresh radish, the golden-bearded ascetic explained his arrival to those present.

2. He said he had grown tired of the city's hurly-burly and conceived the notion of resting in the bosom of nature.

3. His niece, Varya, reverently listened to the words of her erudite uncle, and Pavel Musatov, pouring himself an eighth glass of cherry brandy, bellowed: "And a good thing, too!"

4. He was huge and purple and had penetrated the mysteries of agricultural science, while his brother was thin and pale and packed with knowledge.

1. The landowning Musatov led a life filled with rural grind and rural pleasures.

2. He was no mean drinker and went on sprees, but he kept one eye on the estate.

3. He indulged in amorous intrigues, verified by the scar on his forehead which had appeared after a blow with a stick.

4. He would often say, in a loud voice: "After throwing my money away in Saratov once, I spent a week having to heave great sacks about, loading up steamships."

5. As he said this, he would roll up his sleeves to reveal his hairy arms.

6. Pavel Musatov, the merry master of hospitable Gryazishchi.


1. One hot June day, book in hand, the pale-faced ascetic was taking a walk in the shady avenue.

2. He leafed through an article by Merezhkovich on the union of paganism and Christianity.[21]

3. He sat down on a bench. As he cleaned his nails, he said to himself: "Merezhkovich has committed a series of blunders here. I shall pen an objection to Merezhkovich."

4. Meanwhile Pavel Musatov had sat down unobserved beside him and placed his broad palm over the offending tract.

5. He said through his teeth which gripped a cigar: "Do that later. Now it's time for a bathe."


1. The ascetic plunged into the cold waters by a willow-bush, surrendering to their solace.

2. He bathed with dignity, remembering the holiness of the rite, while his fat brother grew colder on the bank as he stood slapping his naked chest.

3. At last he hurled himself into the water and vanished.

4. It was not a deep dive. Soon his soaking head surfaced, and he snorted: "Marvellous!"

1. Across the endless plains the wind was blowing, whistling down the ravines.

2. It was heading towards Musatov's estate and wailing in grief with the birch trees.

3. They tried to break free into the distance but could not fly away . . . And they bent their heads bitterly.

4. This was time passing, flying into the past on its misty wings.

5. And in the distance the huge sun was dying, entwined in brocade vestments.


1. The golden-bearded ascetic walked quickly up and down the shady avenue.

2. He could see the conclusions of the material he had accumulated, and his black eyes fastened upon space.

3. A straw hat sat on his blonde curls, and he waved a walking-stick with a heavy handle.

4. Much had already been resolved and now he approached the essence.

5. Eternity whispered to her darling child: "Everything returns . . Everything returns . . . All is one . . . all is one . . . in every dimension."

6. "Travel to the west, and you will return to the east . . . The essence of all things is contained in the visible world. Reality is in dreams."

7. "The great sage . . . The great fool . . . All are one . . ."

8. And the trees took up this secret reverie: *everything returns again* . . . And a new rush of time flew into the past . . .

9. And so Eternity teased her darling child, embracing her beloved with her dark outlines, placing her pale, unearthly face against his heart.

10. She covered the eyes of the ascetic with her slender fingers, and he was no longer Musatov but *something* else . . .

11. *What*, *where* and *when* were equally unnecessary as *they* had placed the label of other-wordliness on everything.

1. The ascetic already knew that a great, fateful mystery was rushing towards them from unknown constellations, like a fiery-tailed comet.

2. The orchestra had already struck up the overture. The curtain was due to fly up at any minute.

3. But the culmination of the drama vanished into the distance, because it would still be a thousand years for certain before *they* would untie the Gordian knot binding time and space. Events would follow the channel of time, obeying the principle of sufficient reason.

4. The trees shouted of a new time, and he thought: *"Everything returns again."*

5. He felt both terror and bliss, because he played blind man's buff with the Beloved.

6. She whispered: "All is one . . . No whole, and no parts . . . No distinction between genus and species . . . There is neither reality, nor symbol."

7. "The common fate of the world is played out by each and every one . . . There is both a common and a personal Apocalypse."

8. "There is both a common and a personal Comforter."

9. "Life consists of prototypes . . . One hints at the other, but they are all equal."

10. "When time no longer exists, there will be that which replaces time."

11. "There will be that which replaces space."

12. "These will be *new* times and *new* spaces."

13. "All is one . . . And everything returns . . . The great sage and the great fool."

14. And he joined in: *"Everything returns again and again . . ."* And tears of joy streamed from his eyes.


1. He walked into the fields. A cloud was reddening on the horizon: it looked like a shaven-headed Zaporozhian Cossack frozen in a dance with one leg kicking up towards the sky.

2. But it drifted apart. The horizon was covered in shreds of clouds . . .

Dark-grey patches against a yellow-red background.

3. As if a leopard skin had stretched out in the west.


1. He smiled, having glimpsed his Beloved after day upon day of separation and anguish.

2. While in the distance Pavel Musatov was already speeding along in a racing droshky, cigar between his teeth, holding the reins rakishly.

3. In the distance someone's deep voice sang: "Forgive, forgive my love, my beloved."

4. Pavel Musatov drove off into the aimless distance. Only dust was left rising on the road.

5. A voice sang: "In a far-off foreign land I remember you . . ."

6. A lone peasant, barefoot and dirty, vanished away somewhere amid the cornfields . . .

7. A voice was singing: "Ah, my bitter fate, my bitter fate."

8. A leopard skin stretched out in the west.


1. A lone peasant, barefoot and dirty, vanished away somewhere amid the cornfields . . .


1. The landowner Musatov sat in the cool of the evening.

2. He was resting after the hot day, smoothing out his blond beard.

3. Just now he had been striking his fist against the table and shouting at Prokhor, the village elder: "You're a devil and a blackguard!"

4. While Prokhor bent his head, knitted his brow and shook his enormous beard.

5. And blurted out at this menacing outcry: "I'm sure I don't know about that!" . . .

6. But this had happened a short while ago, and now the corpulent Pavel rested in the cool of the evening.

1. In the brightly lit dining-room his niece Varya was eating wild strawberries. As she speared the berries on a hairpin, she laughed and said: "You, uncle, are like a priest of old . . . You ought to walk around in a robe." . . .

2. He seemed strangely cheerful and would laugh without reason.

3. He was laughing now. "You just wait for us to build our temples . . . As for what we wear, that's nonsense . . . Is this stick of mine not a rod of iron? Is this straw hat of mine not made of gold?"

4. And he raised his hands above his niece and began to declaim in a light-hearted way:

> I am priest supreme
> With white head of hair.
> I shall crown you with garlands
> Sweet-scented and fair.

> And the undying salt
> Of my fiery words spread
> On the glorious, innocent
> Curls of your head.

5. Thus joked Sergey Musatov, the golden-bearded ascetic and prophet.

6. Then he opened the newspaper and read about the embassy of the Tibetan Dalai-Lama.

7. After which he enquired with Varya's mother about the possibility of obtaining a lemon.

8. Then Pavel Musatov read him a lecture about agriculture and failed harvests.

9. They had a peaceful smoke on the open terrace. The moon shone down at them.

1. On that bright blue night their niece Varya was standing by an open window. Her eyes were shining and she was declaiming from a copy of Fet's poems which she was holding in her hands:

> I am priest supreme
> With white head of hair.
> I shall crown you with garlands
> Sweet-scented and fair.

> And the undying salt
> Of my fiery words spread
> On the glorious, innocent
> Curls of your head.

2. But the bright moon vanished and the sky turned blue-black.

3. Only towards the east was it the colour of pale chrysolite.

4. The shadows met, and as they did so, grew thicker. Somewhere in the distance Pavel Musatov was snoring.

5. Sitting in a soft armchair in the dark drawing-room was a familiar woman.

6. Her deathly, immobile countenance radiated white in the darkness.


1. Above the slumbering house the trees were loudly crying out about the new time to come.

2. Gust followed gust; the new time was passing.

3. The new time brought no news. God knows why they were getting so impassioned.

4. And already the light of life had spilled forth on the distant horizon. The drawing-room no longer contained the familiar woman in black with the white countenance.

5. Only on the back of a chair lay someone's forgotten, lace shawl . . .

6. The clamorous time proclaimed: *"Everything returns again."* And already half the sky was turning the colour of pale chrysolite.

7. Unfolded at the very edge of the horizon was a piece of yellow Chinese silk.


1. These were days of hard grind in the fields, days of conclusions drawn from accumulated material; days of forest fires, filling the region around with the fume of smoke.

2. Days when the fates of Russia and the world were being decided: days of objections to Merezhkovich.

3. And more and more defined and clear grew a familiar image with deep-blue eyes and sorrowful lips.

4. This was a snowy-silver banner raised on the fortress at the hour of superstitious expectations.


1. In the morning the golden-bearded ascetic would be drinking tea, as he discussed matters with his brother and joked with his niece.

2. Then he would draw conclusions from material he had accumulated.

3. Then he and his brother would give themselves up to watery consolation and dive amidst the waves. Then encyclicals to his disciples in Moscow and elsewhere would be composed.

4. In them the dogmas of Christianity would be elucidated and allusions made to the possibility of mystical expectations.


1. The number of his Muscovite faithful had widened, and a network of mystics covered Moscow.

2. Each quarter housed its mystic, a fact well known to the local police.

3. They all reckoned with the authority of the golden-bearded ascetic who prepared himself in the country to utter his word.

4. One of them was a specialist on the Apocalypse. He had departed for the north of France to investigate the possible appearance of the coming beast.

5. Another was studying the mystical haze which had thickened over the world.

6. Another was departing in the summer to drink fermented mare's milk; he was attempting to place the question of the resurrection of the dead on a practical footing.[22]

7. Another was touring the monasteries to interview the elders.

8. Another was engaged in a journalistic struggle with the Saint Petersburg mystic, while another was fanning the sparks of grace.

9. Leavenovsky was travelling Russia and delivering lectures replete with winks and nods.

10. The impression was created that he *knew*, but his knowledge was founded upon the golden-bearded prophet.

11. To the unenlightened, his lectures were like a chest of drawers full of locked-away treasure.

12. He had already read six lectures and drafted a seventh.


1. A fancy-looking troika drove up, bearing Pavel Musatov towards his landowning neighbours.

2. Musatov was greeted at the entrance by the familiar family who enquired the reason for Pavel Musatov's long neglect of their hospitable home.

3. To which Pavel Musatov responded with a bow, clicking the heels of his lacquered boots. He raised the tiny hand of his host's wife to his crimson lips and observed: "My erudite brother is staying with us! . . . We talk about this and that, you know . . . And time slips by without our noticing it."

4. To the question why he had not brought his learned brother to visit them, however Musatov gave a sharp, laconic reply: "He spends all his time sitting at home. He's engaged in some wide-ranging research" . . .

5. All this was taken note of by the inquisitive family.


1. In the soft-fruit garden Varya, the niece, was taking a stroll with her friend, Lidiya Verblyudova.

2. Suddenly she threw her arms round Verblyudova's long neck and said: "My dear, you must visit us at Gryazishchi as soon as you can . . . I'll show you my erudite uncle . . ."

3. Verblyudova enquired about the erudite uncle's appearance, and her friend, screwing up her eyes and pulling at the end of her plait, gave a cunning laugh . . .

4. And said nothing in reply.


1. Villages were burning. The zemstvo insurance agent was travelling around the district.

2. As he called in at the various estates, he would be sure to say, as he chewed a piece of ham or covered it with mustard: "And I gather that Pavel Pavlovich is occupied with this brother of his, the scholar . . ."

3. And when he was asked what kind of bird the brother was, he would reply with a meaningful look in his protruding eyes: "He spends all his time sitting at home in Gryazishchi . . . He's engaged in some wide-ranging research!"

1. In the district capital two citizens were having a slap-up meal.

2. The bottles standing on the table were empty, and the eyes of the people who sat there were glazed.

3. One of them grasped the other's knee and said: "Let's down one more each, old man . . . Ha, ha. . . . What's Sergey Musatov's erudition to us? . . . Ha, ha. . . ."

4. To which his companion gloomily replied: "You're right."

1. The house was old and dark-grey. A stone mask hung above the open terrace.

2. Its pale, austere features were suspended motionless, looking a gentle pink in the evening glow.

3. Sitting in state on the open terrace was Pavel Musatov, bathed in scarlet light.

4. His fat stomach swelled beneath his tight-fitting jacket, and his right hand was buried in his beard.

5. His left hand pulled at the ornaments on his watch-chain. Before him on the table were an ash-tray and matches.

6. Two young poplar trees were bending over as if enchanted, tremulous and liquescent with eternal fairy-tales.

7. The anguished cries of lapwings floated up from the river.

8. Frog-eyed Pavel surrendered to sorrowful thoughts in the evening glow.

9. At last he gave a sneeze and walked down the steps of the terrace, after catching sight of a visitor.

10. He was followed by the petrified stone laughter of the mask.

1. A storm was approaching. Loud rumbling and roaring hung over the estate.

2. The strong-rooted trees, gripped by the wind, tried to tear themselves up and away.

3. Columns of heavy rain were approaching and already hung over the ploughed fields.

4. Grey herons passed by over the leaden river.

5. The village schoolmaster was lean and stooping. His sallow face was darker than his bald patch but lighter than his beard, and his snub nose stuck up provocatively from beneath dark-blue spectacles.

6. He was a young man with an affinity for the people.

7. He and Pavel Musatov walked along the avenue of yellowing trees. The teacher's yelping voice contended with the noise of the trees.

8. His sallow face seemed to be grimacing, while his long arms performed absurd movements beneath the leaden vault of the sky.

9. The strong-rooted trees, gripped by the wind, tried to tear themselves up and away.


1. Seated on a painted bench was the golden-bearded ascetic, drawing conclusions from the material he had accumulated.

2. While the teacher was thinking disgustedly: "There sits a *putrefying* mystic!"

3. "He'll be oozing with *holy lamp-oil* and his *dyed-in-the-wool* patriotism nauseates me."

4. The mystic stood up to greet them. He was not putrefying and did not dye wool at all.

5. He was a chemist by profession, and the young schoolmaster shamed himself more than once in his presence through his ignorance of the exact sciences.


1. They were walking off to have supper. The village schoolmaster, who was a great reader, deployed his intellectual army along the front, making sudden sorties against the *putrefying* mystic.

2. There was so far only the occasional cannonade. It had not got as far as case-shot yet.

3. There was still the stock of personal insults in reserve.

4. The pink reflection on the window-panes faded. On the other side of the glass a deathly pale visage looked out at them as they walked.

5. It was as if Eternity the great had pressed herself to the window.

6. But it was a bouquet of white feather-grass, and nothing else.

7. Pavel Musatov was not joining in the argument. Eyes popping out, he sang softly to himself: "Night will pass on wings of mist, a threatening storm-cloud will cover the east!"

8. The storm-cloud was terrible and spread very high up, and beneath it two low, ominously white tendrils of cloud moved away to the side somewhere.

9. On the lawn in front of the house two young poplar trees whispered to the storm, as if enchanted.

10. The reflection of the sunset on the window-panes faded. A bouquet of white feather-grass stood in the window.

11. The village schoolmaster was beginning to blaze up in front of the silent ascetic, while Pavel Musatov sang quietly: "Our shining joy will fade like the sunset, and sorrow arrive like a sudden storm cloud . . ."

12. They had already entered the room and slammed the door when the scraggy dog began to howl, its tail between its legs. Its lean muzzle was turned towards the sky.

13. It was terrified and seemed to be howling: *"Everything returns, everything returns again,"* and the two ominously white tendrils of cloud already hung over the house.

14. The anguished cries of lapwings floated up from the other side of the river.


1. The ascetic said nothing in front of the vociferous schoolmaster, because he was already on the other side of life.

2. This was a waking dream, no less.

3. These were revelations: Eternity teased her favourite and darling child; this eternal badinage sounded like sweet music in the prophet's anguished soul.

4. The prophet knew that he had broken loose from the snares of the three dimensions. People called him a madman: this was a good sign.

5. The prophet already knew that he was a herald of Eternity.

6. He had learned exceeding much, anguished much, removed many veils, fallen greatly in love with Eternity.

7. His dreams were exceeding bright: this was a dream which had risen over Russia like a beloved madness.

8. These were the games which Eternity played with her favourite and darling child.

9. The stone mask above the terrace laughed loudly and was struck dumb in mid-laughter.

10. The anguished cries of lapwings floated up from the other side of the river.

1. This dream had consumed reality with flame and scattered its black ash.

2. "Well, these may be nothing but dreams," thought the prophet, "but let the world play at these dreams for once, let it lose itself in its fantasies."

3. "What would then prevent these dreams from becoming reality?"

4. Thus he thought, and already sweet sorrow made his heart stand still, already other eyes, deep-blue eyes, were staring into his . . . And already the poplar trees moaned in a deep bass voice beneath the weight of Eternity flying by.

5. These were waking dreams soaring past in a roaring stream, and the old poplar trees, raising their bony arms, exulted and cried in a sing-song voice: "Lo! The bridegroom comes at midnight."

1. Outside the windows there was roaring and crying; unknown voices were cursing and screaming and praying.

2. He had seen Moscow, and over Moscow towering clouds with icy summits, and on one cloud the *woman clothed with the sun* was holding in her arms the holy child.

3. And at her feet was spread the supreme prophet and herald of Eternity himself.

4. Diamonds sparkled on his mitre and on his cross, and his golden beard vanished into the cupola of cloud.

5. And the blade of God's sword like lightning from the cloud smote down the unworthy.

6. And in the distance the Antichrist was scurrying back to the north of France.

7. Through the general commotion the old poplar trees, like mighty bishops raising their bony arms, exulted and cried in a sing-song voice: "I see thy mansion, my Saviour."

1. And again, as always, two deep-blue, sorrowful eyes, framed by reddish hair, were staring at the ascetic.

2. There was both smiling and sorrow. There was the question: "Is *this* really true? . . ."

3. They stood by the window out of curiosity and watched the storm.

4. The hail was beating down. Broken-off branches were flying around. Somewhere in the house there was the sound of breaking glass.

5. Here and there the blood-stained blade of a sword briefly appeared, and the stentorian voice of an archdeacon proclaimed: "*Anathema*".

6. This was not yet the Smiter himself, but the sword-blade amidst the clouds.

1. That evening the samovar was hissing. They were sitting in silence around the table.

2. The night was gaping mutely, pressed against the windows, and stared at those who were seated.

3. The ancient clock struck the hour with silken chimes.

4. Their sister was pouring the tea. The golden-bearded ascetic stirred his spoon around in the glass.

5. Varya pulled at the end of her plait. Pavel Musatov took hold of a guitar.

6. Suddenly the stooping schoolmaster began to speak in his yelping voice. Opening his mouth, he launched volley after volley.

7. His snub nose twinkled provocatively at his opponent, while Varya's cheeks suffused with a bright flush.

8. But the jealous schoolmaster was not looking at Varya. Pavel Musatov was, as he fixed new strings onto the old guitar.

9. Then he coughed, gave a sigh and shook his head.

10. But his brother noticed none of this.


1. The samovar was hissing.

2. Somebody was pressed to the windows, with eye-sockets yawning open.

3. But there was nobody there.


1. The schoolmaster cried out: "This is madness!" Varya flashed indignation at the schoolmaster.

2. Pavel Musatov was testing the string with his fat finger.

3. The ascetic's eyes flashed like a thunderstorm, because he remembered the long years spent studying the sciences and philosophy.

4. He snapped with his toneless voice: "If I am mad, it is only because I have passed through all the levels of sanity!"

5. He stood and went over to the window with a yawn.

6. Suddenly Pavel Musatov began to strum the *Persian March* on the guitar.

1. The post was brought. The golden-bearded ascetic read a letter. He said to his brother: "Tomorrow I return to Moscow."

2. The corpulent Pavel was standing behind Varya's back. He said to his brother: "And a good thing, too."

3. His eyes were pointing to the bowed head of his niece.

4. Varya quickly left the room.

5. The schoolmaster's pallid lips curled although he was lighting a *papirosa* impassively.

6. But the ascetic, sunk in his own thoughts, noticed nothing.

7. He went out into the garden.


1. The night dragged on. Bottles clinked. Pavel Musatov was getting the schoolmaster drunk.

2. The schoolmaster's head was slumped on the table. He cried: "Love thy neighbour!"

3. Pavel, who was growing more and more purple, roared with merry laughter. His face glistened with sweat.

4. With one hand he struck the table. With the other he lifted a fragment of wine-glass above his head.

5. There were wine-stains on the table. Flies circled over them.

6. The guitar with its broken strings lay on the floor.


1. In the next room it was dark. This was where Varya was.

2. Her eyes streamed with tears. She was biting a tiny handkerchief.

3. She dropped the handkerchief onto the back of the armchair and went out into the garden.

4. And the handkerchief showed white on the back of the armchair, as if it were someone's face, ominous and deathly-pale.

5. But nobody was there.

1. All night long the ascetic wandered around the garden, enveloped in darkness.

2. His ardent breast heaved with eternal fairy-tales.

3. He had received a letter saying that the family of the coming *beast* had been found, and that as yet the *beast* was not out of swaddling-clothes.

4. As yet it was still a pretty little boy with light-blue eyes, dwelling in the north of France.

5. And the ascetic cried out along nocturnal avenues: "Lo! We shall raise up against the beast the *woman clothed with the sun* as our sacred, snowy-silver banner!"

6. The night-watchman beat his iron plate.


1. Time was soaring over the anguished trees in a roaring stream.

2. Lacerated clouds vanished away towards the misty west.

3. As if someone, evil, were scurrying back to the north of France.

4. And the ascetic knelt in the mud, with his hands raised up towards the sky.

5. He was shouting out ecstatically: *Tat tvam asi*[*23] and beating his breast . . .

6. Day was dawning.


1. And when he entered the house, it was already quite light outside.

2. Dawn drinking was taking place in the dining-room beneath the light of a hanging lamp.

3. Black flies clung to the schoolteacher's lips, and Pavel Musatov staggered over towards his brother.

4. He enveloped him in his drunken breath, as he beat his chest.

5. He was muttering: "That demon, Prokhor . . . In my way . . . Jealous as the Devil" . . .

* "That art thou." (Author's footnote)

115

6. And crashing down onto his knees before the ascetic, he cried: "Sergey, I am madly in love, but *she* is a *paysanne* . . . And the village elder Prokhor is jealous of me, because of her . . ."

7. He was as puce as an aubergine. The ascetic said to him: "Don't drink any more, or you'll go up in flames . . ."


1. The ascetic looked at his brother and the puny schoolmaster. The schoolmaster had black flies clinging to him.

2. The hanging lamp was struggling with the light of day. The guitar lay on the floor.

3. The ascetic was thinking in holy terror: "So this is it — *the deathliness foretold in the Apocalypse!*"

4. Day was dawning. Glancing out of the window, you could seen an old man, the night-watchman, dragging himself into the bushes to sleep.

5. In the east you could see a piece of yellow Chinese silk.

6. And above it the sky was the colour of pale chrysolite.

7. Day was dawning.


1. It was nearly evening. A light rain was falling. Rooks cawed above the white willow trees.

2. Pavel Musatov came out onto the steps to take leave of his brother, Sergey.

3. The troika started off with a jerk, bells jingling. Pavel Musatov remained alone on the steps.

4. He stood there, in a dark-blue, cloth jacket and waving at his brother with his handkerchief.

5. His face was redder than usual. There were bags beneath his eyes.

6. He went into the barn.

1. Women were sweeping the threshing-floor. One of them blushed on seeing Pavel.

2. Pavel did not look at the women.

3. He turned away from Prokhor, the elder, who was standing in front of him, bare-headed.

4. It was cold.


1. That evening he stood on the terrace with Varya and silently smoked a cigar. He said nothing.

2. Varya understood his silent sympathy.

3. Beyond the river someone was singing: "Forgive, forgive my love, my beloved . . ."

4. Eternity's head thrust forward from the wall and hung over the two of them sorrowfully.

5. It was only a mask.


1. A burial veil fluttered above the fields.

2. Travelling along amid the fields was Sergey Musatov, wreathed in autumn mist.

3. He was thinking: "This is nothing . . . These are only reflections of the terror . . ."

4. "Of the misty deathliness approaching from the west . . . But we shall yet fight."

5. "All is not yet ended . . ."

6. In the west the clouds parted. A crimson-fiery finger rose above the misty fields.

7. The ascetic's illuminated face was smiling, although it was cold.

8. But clouds obscured the horizon.

9. The day was going out like a mournful candle.

## PART FOUR

1. Summer flew away on the wings of time. It whirled into the anguished distance.

2. Autumn crept by. And whatever she touched fell to the ground, shedding misty tears.

3. That old hag, winter, had long been trudging the lowlands of Russia, uttering threats in a toothless mumble.

4. By this time Madame Nikolayeva had already spewed out flame from her mouth, like a cannon.*

5. Two millionaires had collapsed, scythed down by Death. A famous writer had all but surrendered his life for the sake of his comrades.


1. There was a great commotion amongst the Moscow mystics: Leavenovsky, egged on by Shipovnikov, the Saint Petersburg mystic,[24] had risen up to wage war on Sergey Musatov.

2. Many words were uttered . . . And people sided with Leavenovsky, who was arising in splendour.

3. Leavenovsky's party merged with the party of the cunning Shipovnikov . . . And they were joined by Merezhkovich.

4. Those who remained closed ranks more tightly around the golden-bearded one, turning their hopeful gaze towards him.

5. They waited for signs.


1. From Voronukhin Hill the entire horizon was visible. A triangle of fire shone from the dark clouds.

* See the newspapers for June. (Author's footnote)

2. Crowds of people assembled and saw in this a great sign.

3. It was a long time before they dispersed, trying to make sense of it.


1. One person arrived at the house of another, rosy from the walk.

2. Without removing his galoshes, he shouted from the entrance-hall: "Holy days are dawning over Moscow! . . . We must go and catch a glimpse of them, brother, this frosty evening! . . ."

3. "A new star has begun to shine in the sky!"

4. "With its rising we await the resurrection of the dead . . . The deceased Vladimir Solov'yov was seen recently, riding fur-hatted in a cab with his collar pulled up!"

5. "Vladimir Solov'yov threw his fur-coat open before the one who *saw*, revealed himself and cried down from the cab: 'The end is already nigh: that which has been longed for will soon come to pass'."

6. They both found themselves out in the frosty cold, and the frosty cold tinted their noses.

7. They began to walk quickly after turning into an empty by-street. Like two experienced bloodhounds they followed the scent of grace.

8. They peeped in at windows and other people's courtyards. And their eyes gleamed.

9. Chimneys howled. The gates of buildings creaked. Denuded trees whistled as they contorted their branches.

10. The Milky Way descended lower than it should. Like a white mist it hung above their heads.


1. The snow crunched beneath the feet of passers-by. Where during the day there had been a puddle, there was now bare ice . . . And a passing upstart tumbled head-over-heels, parodying European civilisation.

2. A pair of fast carriage horses whirled her along the illuminated streets . . . And she, luminous herself, fastened her eyes on the white snow.

3. The frost had tinged her cheeks with red, and eternal aspiration was reflected in her eyes.

4. Her coral-coloured lips grew pale.

5. Yesterday there had been a party, and today preparations were being made for a ball . . . And now she surrendered herself to the rapture of snow.

6. Like an empress whirling along on the wings of fantasy, and the wind whistled, enveloping her in its chill.

7. These were eternal stories about that which is not, and which might have been, but had not come about.

8. And her gaze was fixed on the fathomless, and the fathomless shone, reflected in her gaze.

9. And here she was, flying along like a sacred vision, raising a flurry of snow.


1. The Church of the Burning Bush was locked. All the same they opened it from within.

2. They stood in the porch, noticed by nobody.

3. One wore an enormous fur-coat and hat, and the other was dressed in a quilted coat and a peaked winter cap.

4. Both were tall and lean and had a stoop. One looked like a church-deacon, apart from his gold spectacles, which he had removed from his nose and was wiping with a handkerchief.

5. A lion's mane of grey hair was escaping from under his peaked cap. His grey beard was trimmed.

6. He looked at the bright star which trailed a thread of gold and said, screwing up his eyes: "Well, Vladimir Sergeyevich? It is the day-star bursting into flame!"

7. Good-natured wrinkles creased his mouth and eyes. He locked the church.

8. The two began to walk along Poluektov Lane in animated conversation.

1. They were seated on a snow-covered bench in the Devichy Field. They threw back their heads to look at the sky, risking the loss of their hats in the snow.

2. They examined the sky with their good-natured, short-sighted eyes.

3. They looked up at the Milky Way, and the Milky Way, like a white mist, shone with past youth and dreams beyond recall.

4. The one wearing the fur-hat said in a muffled bass: "They've seen nothing yet!"

5. In the distance bare besoms of trees shook their black arms, begging for a breath of holy wind.


1. For a long time they were silent, as they enacted the mystery. At last the one in the peaked cap and quilted coat suddenly started to yell like a child.

2. He struck his hand against the frozen bench and, shaking his lion's mane and grey beard, cried out: "Hey! . . . But they shouldn't behave like this, Vladimir Sergeyevich! They'll completely compromise us with these absurd games of theirs! . . . It is, after all, quite ridiculous!"

3. Whereupon he began to demolish Sergey Musatov's conclusions, while the one beside him burst into raucous laughter, like a madman. His feet thumped the ground with merriment, as he threw open his fur-coat.

4. His black, grey-flecked beard blew in the wind, and the trees shook their black arms, begging for a breath of holy wind.

5. The Milky Way, like a white mist, shone with past youth and dreams beyond recall.

6. At last, controlling his laughter, he said: "It doesn't matter, Bars Ivanovich:[25] the first pancake always turns out badly."

7. Two parishioners shuddered at this holy laughter, but they did not trouble to look at the face of the one who was laughing.

8. If they had looked, tenderness and fear would have moved their troubled souls.

9. They would have recognised old friends.

1. They sat on the bench for a long time yet, quietly conversing together.

2. Then they walked around Moscow, peeping in at the windows of friends: pressing themselves against the cold window-panes and making the sign of the cross over their brothers.

3. More than one friend heard the snow-storm tapping at the window. More than one friend raised confused eyes towards the nocturnal windows, screwing up his eyes in the light of the lamp.

4. He did not know, after all, that old friends were knocking and making the sign of the cross over him with their ghostly hands.

5. Thus the two wanderers roamed around Moscow.

6. At last, with a sorrowful sigh, they cast a valedictory glance across the neighbourhood . . . They withdrew until their next encounter in joy.

7. In the Novodevichy Convent, among the graves, they shook hands and parted, each to his own rest.


1. Sitting enthroned at a wide table was the founder of neo-Christianity himself, the one who had drawn conclusions from accumulated material, who had passed through all the levels of sanity, who had accepted at the highest level the crown of holy madness.

2. Beside him sat a mysterious personage who had returned from India —a participant in esoteric mysteries.

3. He was a sun-bronzed man, quite hairless, with a long nose and a gold ear-ring in one ear.

4. There was also a theosophist there, with a red moustache, arrived from London and wearing a fashionable tie.

5. There was another familiar person there, too, frozen in an affected pose. He listened a lot and said little.

6. The beaming host walked amongst his guests, rubbing his white hands, while the mystics encircled him, asking: "Who's that sitting in that affected pose?"

7. To which the host replied quietly, putting his finger to his lips: "He's a former Kantian, disillusioned with his ideals . . . A seeker after truth who has spent time in a lunatic asylum, but who didn't find it there, either . . ."

8. "They recently released him, and he has come here to acquaint himself with our views. We shall lure him into our net . . ."

9. The mystics looked at the seeker after truth from time to time, and he at them.


1. In one corner people disputed the sighting of Solov'yov, and in another a pillar of mysticism was teaching people how to raise the dead.

2. He swore he had expended much labour in this direction and had already achieved results of sorts.

3. People were doubtful.

4. New guests were arriving with faces red from the frost. Father Ioann entered in a black, silk cassock and smoothed his satiny white hair.

5. He sat down silently at the green table and silently surveyed the noisy gathering. In his deep-blue eyes, the eyes of a child, you would have seen sadness.


1. Sergey Musatov was saying: "It has approached . . . It has returned again . . . It has begun . . . "

2. "You all witnessed it when you looked at the star, shining now, as it did one thousand nine hundred years ago . . ."

3. "Now it is shining for us again!"

4. The man with the ear-ring in his ear exchanged glances with the red-moustached theosophist, and Musatov continued:

5. "He was growing up in peace and quiet, until the hour when his appearance to the world became imperative . . . I have been expecting his appearance from hour to hour . . ."

6. "But I shall not mislead you regarding the chalice from which it is our lot to drink: it is the struggle with the Coming Beast."

7. "Now it is maturing in Western Europe."

8. "Now the whole world will look with trembling towards the countries embracing Belgium, Holland and the north of France . . ."

9. "Therefore may the mother of our white standard-bearer be sanctified — the *woman clothed with the sun!*"


1. The speech of the prophet was short. His words more than strange. But even stranger was the voice of the mysterious personage from India.

2. "Slumbering dreams . . . I am familiar with it . . . I *know* . . . You are drifting in dreams, as you curse deceptive reality . . ."

3. "But after all, dreams are the same reality, the same deception . . . You have not yet slept without dreams . . ."

4. He threw back his shaven head, ear-ring glittering, and cawed like a black raven to the assembled company: "How long, how long before they recognise thee, o Karma!"


1. The mystics went off to drink tea, the priest looked at his watch, the theosophist smoothed his red moustache, and the mysterious personage from India plunged into abstract contemplation . . .

2. The prophet raised his head, looked at the frosted patterns on the windows and said in a steady voice, in reply to these objections: "A dreamless sleep, is that all it is?"

3. "It would be strange if we had not passed through the level of dreamless sleep . . ."

4. "But when we caught sight of that which no-one before us had seen — then we *awoke and returned* . . ."

5. Father Ioann removed his black spectacles from his pocket, placed them before his dim-sighted, deep-blue eyes and began to look through the papers which lay on the table.

6. Musatov had turned around and awaited objections from the shaven man with the ear-ring in one ear, but the man was not even aware of Musatov.

7. He had plunged into abstract contemplation, reflecting on the condition of dreamlessness.

8. The priest did make an objection, saying modestly: "You are mistaken!"

9. And when the ascetic flared up and was ready to fall upon the turbulent priest, eyes flashing like black diamonds, —

10. Then the priest was not frightened at all, but removed his glasses and examined the ascetic attentively.


1. At this point the theosophist of Jewish extraction intervened. Twirling his red moustache, he struck up a purring tune.

2. In his fashionable tie he resembled a crafty cat, as he shook the prophet's hand and explained: "You and I have a great deal in common . . . We are fighting for the same thing . . ."

3. "Our watchword is *pansynthesis* . . . And we do not separate morality from knowledge. Religion, science, philosophy differ quantitatively, but not qualitatively . . ."

4. But the piqued prophet disengaged his hand and haughtily remarked: "We know your concern for synthesis . . . We know what that is about . . ."

5. "We have no need for gnostic fantasies, and your friends, the Hindus, hold no allure."

6. "We are not children. We love pure gold, not false glitter . . ."

7. "Building a temple, you compare the cupola, crowned with a cross, with the foundations . . . Who has ever seen such a building?"

8. "Carry on co-ordinating, but we shall subordinate . . ."

9. "All the same, you still have some things to talk about . . Do drop in for a cup of tea . . ."

10. The golden-bearded prophet stopped at this point, because he was thrown into a tremble by a cherished image: it was the *woman clothed with the sun.*

11. *This* he saw . . . And he caught the deep-blue eyes of Ioann staring at him, the eyes of a child, shining with reproach.

12. But the priest pretended to examine the papers . . .

1. Studded all over with diamonds, *she* stood at the frosted window.

2. Starlight shone somewhere beyond, and she, in a white dress lit up by stars and moon, was like a sacred vision.

3. She was going to the ball, but at this moment stood by the window and remembered that which was not, and which might have been, but had not come about.

4. Her soul mourned, and as it mourned, grew joyful . . . And in mourning, rose up to the sky! . . .

5. . . . And at last a diadem of twelve stars flashed on her head . . . And tearing herself away from the frosted window, she continued her preparations for the ball . . .

6. And in her deep-blue eyes there was such brightness and such power that two stars hurtled down from the moonlit sky, trembling with fellow-feeling . . .

1. The theosophist had already left in a cab, taking with him the mysterious personage from India . . .

2. The mysterious personage from India yawned impassively. While the theosophist expounded for his edification.

3. "It's all nonsense . . . They are going against common sense . . ."

4. "Common sense teaches us to be patient: not for another five years will unexpected things be possible . . ."

5. "Another five years . . . Meanwhile it's impossible to talk positively about anything before 1906."

6. The mysterious personage from India listened impassively to the voice of common sense . . .

7. It yawned.

1. After donning his roomy galoshes and wrapping himself in his fur-coat, Father Ioann was already on his way out into the moonlit night.

2. . . . He was thinking: "These are playthings . . . But dangerous ones."

3. There was a slight frost. The snow crunched beneath his feet.

4. Deserted courtyards sang with the secret dream: *"Everything returns . . . Everything returns again."* And the priest wrapped himself more tightly in his coat.

5. He *knew* a great deal but was biding his time.


1. During the night people were asleep. Someone had a dream.

2. A Hindu stood on the banks of the Ganges, a lotus flower in his hands.

3. The Hindu was preaching: "Our knowledge is not false glitter, but pure gold . . ."

4. "And we have had our own Kant, our own Schelling, our own Hegel, our own positivists . . ."

5. "So what else! . . . You *do* amaze us!"

6. "Learn wisdom from Shri Shankarachariya and Patanjali! . . . What do you know of the *brahman* of Vedanta or the *purushas* of Samkhya . . ."[26]

7. Thus the sleeper's Hindu preached and was reflected in the water, upside down, a lotus flower in his hands.


1. Shrove-tide arrived. Rich pancakes were baked for the people of Moscow.

2. The days were snowy. Jingling troikas vanished in the whirling columns of blizzard.

3. They awaited the appearance of the holy child. They knew not who the child was, nor who was clothed with the sun.

4. Their knowledge was founded upon the ascetic.

5. He had learned exceeding much, anguished much, removed many veils, fallen greatly in love with Eternity.

6. Eternity had lit up a new star for her darling and favourite child, and now the whole world wondered at the marvel.

7. Eternity had pointed to the child emblazoned with the sign and the woman clothed with the sun.

8. And while he was thinking this and not thinking this, the blizzards rose up and died down.

9. Troikas, their bells jingling, vanished into the flurry of snow.

10. Something tender whispered: "I have not forgotten you, my dear ones . . . Soon we shall see each other!"


1. One was sitting in the house of the other. Both had plunged into the theosophical depths.

2. One was saying to the other: "White light is the light of consolation, representing the harmonious merging of every colour . . ."

3. "Purple light is the sacred light of the Old Testament, and red is the symbol of martyrdom."

4. "One must not confuse *red* and *purple*. That is where people come to grief."

5. "Purple is the noumenal colour, and red the phenomenal."

6. Both sat in the theosophical depths. One was talking nonsense to the other.


1. Dawn blazed up through the dense white fog, breaking into rosy laughter. The ascetic woke up and, with a yawn, stretched out his hand for the clock on his bedside table.

2. He jumped out of bed and, remembering the meeting he was to have, blew a kiss to the frosty dawn.

3. He was laughing, like a little *child*.

4. Then he was handed a letter from the north of France. He tore open the envelope and read it, rubbing his sleepy eyes.

1. They wrote to inform him that the *Beast* had been stricken with a stomach disorder and had surrendered its soul to God before attaining the age of five, having taken fright at its terrible task.

2. The ascetic tugged at his golden beard in confusion, whispering: "But what about the Apocalypse?"

3. Donning his pince-nez, he began to read the letter again.

4. At last he quickly began to get dressed, and his hands trembled with agitation.

5. While at the window above the white snow the crimson dawn was laughing loudly, as mad and harum-scarum as a little *child*.


1. On that white day a certain person was talking to the old woman, Mertvago, and listening to the intimate songs of the snow-storm.

2. Through the window you could see the snow-covered courtyard, and hanging down from the edges of the roofs were gigantic icicles.

3. It was a person neither old, nor young, but *passive* and *knowing*, and in his conversation with the old woman he was expressing his dissatisfaction with the behaviour of the Moscow mystics.

4. He said that disappointment awaited them, because they had chosen the false path.

5. Regretful and melancholy, he stared with clouded gaze at the pale snow twisting and whirling, as it hid the icicles from view.

6. He seemed to be saying to himself: "Well, there you are, Lord! They are *unable to see themselves!*"

7. But old woman Mertvago did not want to understand this intimate fairy-tale of his and advised him to make a complaint.


1. In the drawing-room stood the fairy-tale. She looked at the visiting-card and said: "Ask him to come in . . ."

2. Mechanically smoothing her reddish hair, she mechanically went with enchanting smile to meet the golden-bearded prophet.

3. The leader of the neo-Christians was pale. Black diamonds did not gleam from beneath his lowered eye-lashes.

129

4. The downy gold of his hair fell onto his pensive forehead. In his long-skirted frock-coat he appeared wrapped in mystery.

5. He exclaimed to himself: *"The woman clothed with the sun!"* In his mind's eye he lifted up his hands, enacting the mystery.

6. While the fairy-tale stood before him with a questioning smile. Surprised by the ascetic's arrival, she politely asked him to sit down.

7. The ascetic announced that he had come to decline the offer made by the centaur that he should give a lecture on mysticism at the charity evening in aid of widows and elderly ladies.

8. His time was taken up, it was quite impossible for him to burden himself with unnecessary work.

9. The fairy-tale listened nonchalantly to his announcement, wishing to send him on his way as quickly as possible.


1. "And now we shall put on this cylinder," said the wiry general and, wiping the dust from the wax cylinder wth a soft brush, inserted it and set the phonograph in motion.

2. Guttural groans began to fly out from the horn: "O-oh! If I could o-only tell you of my siffering so lo-onely . . ."


1. The sunset laughed loud over Moscow, and Musatov said in agitation: "Don't be amazed . . . I have something important to tell you . . . When may I come to see you? . . ."

2. He blushed, and the astonished fairy-tale said to him impatiently: "But we are 'at home' daily between two and four!"

3. At that moment the door-curtain parted. A pretty boy with deep-blue eyes and shoulder-length curls ran in.

4. This, of course, was the boy-child who was to rule the nations with a rod of iron.

5. "Charming boy," said Sergey Musatov, making superhuman efforts not to give himself away. "What's his name?"

6. But the fairy-tale gave a laugh, turned her emblazoned face towards the child, adjusted its curls and said with mock severity: "Nina, how many times have I told you not to come in here without being asked."

7. Nina pouted her lips, and the fairy-tale cheerfully remarked to the ascetic: "My husband and I dress her as a boy."

8. The sunset laughed like a little child, red all over and quite mad.

9. The edifice, built on shaky foundations, had collapsed in ruins. The walls had come crashing down, raising columns of dust.

10. A knife had pierced the loving heart, and scarlet blood flowed into the cup of sorrows.

11. The heavens rolled up like a redundant scroll, while the fairy-tale with charming civility carried on a genteel conversation.

12. All the blood had rushed to the head of the bamboozled prophet, and scarcely able to stay on his feet, he hastened to take his leave of the puzzled fairy-tale.


1. "And now, if I put on this cylinder, you'll be able to hear Pyotr Nevsky, the jolly accordion-player and singer," cried the wiry general, full of enthusiasm.

2. And already guttural groans flew from the horn, words full of banality, and after each verse Pyotr Nevsky would repeat to the sound of his accordion: "Jolly good, jolly good. Really that is jolly good . . ."


1. "The first pancake always turns out badly," said the cook in his white hat, as he looked at the failed pancake.

2. "Well, never mind. Perhaps the others will turn out all right . . ." And with these words he threw the pancake to the greedy dog.


1. In Savost'yanov's bakery they were enquiring whether there was any leaven in reserve, and when they discovered that the leaven was all used up, they made arrangements to buy in some new.

1. The matinée performance at the Popular Arts Theatre was coming to an end . . . Under cover of mist the white-haired dreamer was leading his white lady towards the glaciers so as to clothe her with the sun.

2. An avalanche rushed down in a great roar of dust and bore them away to eternal rest.[27]

3. And Eternity herself stood on the crag arrayed in black, and her voice sounded out like an over-stretched string.

4. This was not reality, but a performance . . . And *they* quickly rang down the curtain because there was nothing more to perform.


1. One sat at the house of the other. Both were saying clever things.

2. One was saying to the other: "If red light is synonymous with God the Father, and red and white synonymous with Christ, then what is white synonymous with?

3. "We have already lived through the red and seen Him that came *not by water only, but by blood also* . . . Now we shall see the third kingdom, the *white* kingdom, the *new* word . . ."

4. The one enthusiastically waved his finger in front of the other's nose . . . The other believed the first.


1. Popovsky's had toothache . . .


1. Standing at the corner was a beggar, his coat thrown open wide, drawing the attention of passers-by to his nakedness.

2. A student approached from the left, and the ascetic from the right . . . And for both of them the beggar pointed his finger at his nakedness.

3. The student despised private charity, and Musatov did not notice the beggar.

4. Eternity whispered to her darling and favourite child: "I was playing a game . . . . Well, you can do the same as well . . . All of us play games . . ."

5. In the face of Eternity's blandishments, the bamboozled prophet maintained a proud silence. He pulled up his beaver-fur collar.

6. It had not been the *woman clothed with the sun*. It had been a fraudulent fairy-tale. But why had her image so burnt Sergey Musatov with fire? . . .

7. He whispered: "It can't be! It can't be!" And the beggar dragged after him and, holding his fetid breath, tried to thrust his hand into Musatov's pocket.

8. For ten years the beggar had struggled with capitalism by regulating private property and had spent time in prison more than once.


1. And already it was evening. The inhabitants of Moscow were resolutely getting up to mischief.

2. Crooks from the Khitrovsky Market and other riff-raff were milling around the doss-houses.

3. Tambourines jingled at the booths, and a painted clown would regularly scurry out into the cold to perform contortions in front of the assembled company, enticing people to enter the haunt of affectation.

4. This gaiety differed from the real kind which is harmonious, like a well-tuned orchestra . . . *These* were lifeless wood-shavings, however.

5. Someone was banging a big brass drum, and the roundabout whirled round wildly, its fiery strips of red calico, gold tinsel and coloured lights twinkling.

6. The wooden lions bared their teeth, and sitting on them were men in peaked caps, chewing sunflower seeds.

7. Suburban restaurants glimmered with their ominous lights, trying with gas and electricity to conceal their deathly pallor.

8. At Omon's Theatre naked songstresses screeched obscenitites.


1. A terrible necrosis hung over the city. Flaming torches of horror and delirium flickered down both sides of the streets.

2. The feverish traffic could not conceal the horror and merely revealed the suppurations even further.

3. Avenging angels seemed to hover over the city beating their invisible wings.

1. They awaited the *comforter*, but it was the *avenger* who approached . . .

1. Lit up by the lights of street-lamps, the prophet still wandered the streets.

2. He dropped into a restaurant to drown in wine the sorrow that was gnawing at him.

3. He was doing this for the first time. He remembered his brother, Pavel.

4. As he swallowed iced champagne in a private room, he kept on exclaiming: "It can't be . . . It can't be . . . Where are we flying to?"

5. "Isn't it time to stop? . . ."

1. A concert was in progress. Shlyapin was singing.[28] He sang about fate and how it threatens.

2. They called Shlyapin back on stage. They talked about Shlyapin. Shlyapin walked out to their curtain-calls.

3. Twisting his chestnut-coloured side-whiskers, purple-faced Nebarinov held forth during the intervals, exchanging bows with those who were there, remembering those who were not.

4. The enchanting fairy-tale smiled at the aristocratic old man, as if she were an angel and the auditorium — the Kingdom of Heaven.

5. Tall, grey-haired Kandislavsky was there with his black moustache, while the corpulent centaur had taken the arm of an elegant, dark-haired man with twisted moustaches and was leading him through the cultivated throng. As he did so, people around him whispered: "Look, there goes the famous writer, Leavenovsky!"

6. There was a rustle of silk dresses.

1. But everyone went back to their seats, and a lady singer emerged, studded with diamonds.

2. The fairy-tale listened to the singer, oppressed by life's vanity.

3. Today there was an official dinner, and tomorrow a morning reception, but now she did not have to smile, but could exist in fantasies.

4. The singer, sparkling with diamonds, thrust her neck forward as she sang and strained every nerve: "My erstwhile joy, where'er art thou? Ah, spent am I and weary now!"

1. Motionless as a statue, she stood there in her black head-dress, and in her raised hands could be seen the eternal rosary.

2. Her dainty face, as pale as marble, had frozen in a tearless cry. Like the fairy-tale, she too was full of anguish beneath the moonless sky.

3. Both were pining, both were yearning, both were reaching out to the world beyond.

4. Both shared the same sorrow.

5. As it passed over the peaceful cloister, the wind rattled the metal wreaths on the snow-covered graves . . . And the wreaths resounded: "My erstwhile joy, where'er art thou? Ah, spent am I and weary now!"

1. Drunk and red-faced, he paid the bill and, swaying slightly, walked out of the restaurant.

2. The image of the *woman clothed with the sun* laughed into his face. He could hear the familiar words: "My husband and I dress her as a boy . . ."

3. At this point the drunken Musatov slipped and tumbled head-over-heels, parodying European civilisation.

4. As he got to his feet, he shook off the snow and whispered: "Where

are we flying to? . . . It can't be, it can't be!"

5. He pulled up his beaver-fur collar.

6. And above him hung deathliness, and he could hear the beating of invisible wings.

7. He could hear vengeful cries.


1. *They* pointed out the open door to him. He heeded *their* advice.

2. Do not blame him, esteemed readers! It was *they* themselves who whispered to him: "Here you will resolve your misunderstanding."

3. And he entered that infernal place, and the dozing door-keeper did not trouble to ask his business.

4. *They* pointed out the door, and it was *they* who had nailed a name-plate to the door.


1. Above the desk there hung a lamp, just as you will find in any government office.

2. On the desk were a carafe and a glass.

3. Sitting on the floor was an obese man with a red nose and red hair, dressed in nothing but a white night-cap and underclothes.

4. He repeatedly raised his index finger as he lectured clearly and coherently to an invisible audience.


1. "Let us assume that I have at my disposal a metal flue."

2. "I hammer it into the ground after covering the opening with a damper. I bring along some half-wits, remove the damper in front of their noses and reveal the hole."[29]

3. The fat, eyebrowless man finished his lecture and began to look around smugly. But at that point the door burst open with a crash. A lean, pretentious-looking person with black, beetling brows, a wild expression and tousled hair jumped in from outside.

4. He was also dressed in under-clothes with nothing on his feet. He

began to cough consumptively when he saw that Musatov had walked in. He jumped over to the groaning lump of flesh and, in a whisper, ordered him to be quiet.

5. Whereupon our discalced orator cried out in a great voice: "Petrusha, let me shout out just one more little horror!"


1. "You have probably appeared in order to find out some secrets, my dear fellow. I am at your service." With these words he sat Musatov down and, hand pressed to his chest to control his dry cough, settled himself in front of him . . .

2. "People seldom call in here. I find that unforgivably thoughtless. The fact that you are seeing us does you honour, sir."

3. "Well, sir? . . . What have you got to say?"

4. Meanwhile, the dumbfounded Musatov, having realised *what it was all about*, asked a question. "What are the greatest truths in the universe?"

5. "Everything increases in refinement, as it grows more specialised . . ."

6. "I already know that very well for myself," remarked the disappointed Musatov. Whereupon his affected confidant was suddenly filled with indescribable enthusiasm.

7. "Is it possible?" he cried. "Have you really got as far as *that*?"

8. "Of course. Every fourth-form grammar-schoolboy in our country knows *that*."

9. "But surely you can't know yet that everything returns?" cried the poseur, with explanatory gestures.

10. "But of course! I know that too," said Musatov, becoming irritated. "And that isn't what I came to find out, either . . ."

11. "In that case, there is nothing further I can teach you, most learned one!" squealed Peten'ka, a malicious grin on his face as he clasped his hands together in mock astonishment . . .

12. "But maybe I should just tell you the mystery of mysteries, to put your mind at rest: *there are no mysteries*."

13. The hanging lamp was smoking away, just as you will find in any government office. The reek of soot was making Musatov sneeze.

14. Musatov had grown quite exasperated with this poseur's pack of lies and, thumping his fist down onto the table, was surprised to find himself yelling: "You can't fool me, my friends!"

15. Drunk and discourteous as he now was, he resembled his brother Pavel.


1. You dare not do anything *but* believe my words," hissed Pyotr, beginning to whistle like the autumn wind. "Because I am the *essence*, I am *the thing in itself!*" he went on, bending his menacing face down towards Musatov and spattering him with saliva, like a torrent of rain.

2. Musatov gulped down several glasses of water and clutched his head in his hands. He was burning, as if in a fever. Meanwhile, the words of the fat man, who had begun to speak again, reverberated in his ears: "Let us assume that it is as hot as in Africa . . . . I strip off all my clothes and wallow about on an ant-hill . . . Thousands of tiny insects bite into my body!"

3. The fat man was crawling all over the floor and laughing, laughing to the point of helplessness.


1. "Could this really be the world of the fourth dimension revealing itself to me?" thought Musatov, terrified at the *modus operandi* of this world that surrounded him. "Yes, yes, yes, yes, yes!" prompted the essence of things in the shape of Petrushka. "A million times yes! This is the so-called world of the fourth dimension! . . . The point is that it doesn't exist at all . . . People have explored far and wide, travelled into every corner of the three dimensions. They have discovered all there is to discover, but this hasn't appeased their thirst. Like incurable alcoholics they need more and more vodka, even though the vodka itself is all finished and the bottle quite empty . . . So they have gone on to invent this fantasy of the fourth dimension the other side of their wall . . . And they began to beat against the wall in a desire to break through into this fourth dimension . . . They should be careful!" he trumpeted in a voice so loud that the walls shuddered,

while his gleaming teeth and the whites of his eyes glittered dazzlingly. "They should be careful, because the *Avenger* is alive! . . . Hark! You can hear the sound of his wings beating ominously above us, as over Gomorrah on the day of its destruction!"

2. "But *is* there anything behind the wall?" whispered Musatov, who had turned deathly pale.

3. "Just such a room with just such wallpaper as you'll see in any government office, with just such an eccentric as yourself hammering at the wall with his fists, thinking there is something on the other side . . . He should be careful because the Tormentor, like a giant, hairy spider, is spinning his webs ready to gorge on the madman's fiery blood!"

4. At the end of this utterance Pyotr's protuberant brows knitted together, and green lightning flashed in his wild eyes with terrifying fury. But these flames were quickly extinguished, and as he closed his eyes up tightly, he looked for all the world like an extinct volcano.

5. Pallid as death, he sat there in deep silence.


1. "Well and what *about* death?" Musatov was enquiring.

2. The threatening Pyotr revived, resurrected himself. "Death involves transferring the inhabitant of room no. 10,000 to room no. 10,001, assuming that all the proper documents are to hand," he said.

3. The hanging lamp was slowly going out when a tail-coated servant brought the gentlemen a glass of tea and some bagels.


1. "Can there be a union between West and East?"

2. And Pyotr the Threatener said in reply: "What sort of union could there be? After all, the West stinks of putrefaction, and the only reason the East doesn't stink is because it already decomposed ages and ages ago!"

3. "But who does the future smile upon?"

4. At this point a slight difficulty occurred: the essence of things grabbed hold of his underpants which were slipping down and squatted on the floor in amazement. Then, beating his hand against his high

forehead, he began to shake his head in reproach: "Well! What's wrong with you, my friend?! . . . You have penetrated our mysteries and yet don't know such an elementary truth!"

5. Then the essence of things poured the carafe of cold water on to Musatov's head, repeating as he did so: 'What about the Negro? . . . What about the Negro?"

6. "Ah yes, the Negro," said the prophet in a weak voice, adjusting his hair which was wet from the water.

7. "The Negro, the Negro! Of course, the Negro! . . . The swarthy, rosy-lipped Negro — there you have the future master of the world!"

8. At this point Musatov let his head drop onto the table and he froze in an access of drunken despair.


1. The entertaining fat one was delivering a new lecture to his invisible audience.

2. "I cut open a stomach . . . I extract and clean the intestines . . . After cutting off the requisite piece of intestine, I sew the amputated ends together,

3. And it's in the bag," he said enthusiastically, finishing his lecture, while the barefoot Pyotr was already trampling on him, whispering feverishly: *You're up to your old tricks again*, you white-haired sinner!"

4. But the fat man pleaded with him piteously: "Pierre, my friend, do let me shout out just one more little horror!"

5. To which Pyotr replied in a kind of calm preceding a storm, not auguring well at all: "Be quiet and don't open up old wounds!"

6. But Musatov was no longer able to hear, as he was running down the stairs.

7. He was whispering: "What is this, Lord? What on earth is this?"

8. He nearly knocked over a swarthy Negro who was walking proudly along the illuminated street with an elegant top-hat and spruce appearance.

9. The inquisitive Negro looked about him and thought insolently: "Well, what's this Moscow compared to Chicago!"

10. Under the influence of this dreadful thought his thick-lipped face broke into a smile.

11. And circling over this Sodom in search of stinking carrion were threatening vultures, rejoicing in the longed-for necrosis.


1. After Musatov's departure the barefoot eccentrics were seated peacefully at the desk. Each was stirring his spoon around in a glass of tea.

2. A strange feature had formed on their heads: two pairs of genuine horns, grown from God knows where or why . . .

3. The fat one was saying to the thin one: "But you're a real expert, Peten'ka, a real fraud, and a real liar!"

4. As he said this, he tittered.

5. But Pyotr did not share his merriment, and he growled: "He may well guess where his strength lies . . . *They are cunning, after all . . .*"


1. I think, gentlemen, that you would have glimpsed two figures sitting on graves.

2. Both were tall and lean and had a stoop. The beard of one blew in the wind and beneath his eye-lashes, so black they seemed to be outlined in charcoal, two grey eyes stared out sorrowfully.

3. The other was wearing a peaked winter cap and gold spectacles.

4. The one said to the other: "I feel sorry for Musatov even so, Bars Ivanovich, for all his arrogance and self-assurance!"

5. But the other one cried out: "Hey! But you can't let them get away with every absurdity, Vladimir Sergeyevich!"

6. "After all, Musatov's conclusions are the conclusions of a clod-hopper."

7. Perhaps I only thought I saw this, gentlemen, and there was only a beautiful, but anguished, woman standing among the graves sobbing tearlessly and with an eternal rosary and wearing a black head-dress . . .

1. That night everyone slept. Rich and poor. Clever and stupid.

2. All slept.

3. Some slept in contorted positions, some slept with their mouths open. Others looked dead.

4. All slept.

5. And already the white day was angrily begging to be let in at the windows. This seemed to be a new summons to the exhausted.

6. An inducement to new pretence.


1. In the morning the bell was ringing, because the gaiety had ended and the great despond approached.

2. In the markets dried mushrooms were being sold, and there was soft slush everywhere.

3. Dampness dripped from the roofs. The ominous sky threatened a misty spring.


1. Sitting in his study was a celebrated scientist, sprawling in a leather armchair and sharpening a pencil.

2. His white hair fell negligently onto the high forehead, renowned for many remarkable discoveries in the field of science.

3. Standing before him in an elegant pose was a young professor of philology, smoking an expensive cigar.

4. The celebrated scientist was saying: "No, I am not satisfied with modern youth! . . . I find them dishonest, and this is why."

5. "Armed with the exact sciences they could repel these various fabrications of mysticism, occultism, demonism, etc. . . . But they prefer to flirt with obscurantism . . ."

6. "Their souls have been invaded by a love of falsehood. The pure light of truth is an irritant to their weak eyes."

7. "All this would be excusable if only they believed in these absurdities . . . But that's the whole point: they don't . . ."

8. "All they seem to need is intoxicating twaddle . . ."

9. The young philology professor had leant his elbows on the back of an armchair and respectfully heard the white-haired celebrity out, although his lips were twisting in a scarcely visible smile.

10. He objected smugly: "All this is true, but you'll agree that this reaction against scientifc formalism is purely temporary."

11. "Sweeping aside their exaggerations and radical inconsistencies, we still see the same aspiration to truth here."

12. "After all, Spencer's differentiation and integration embrace only the formal side of life's phenomena, permitting other inter-pretations . . ."

13. "After all, no-one has any objections to raise against the continuity of evolution. But it's a question of seeking out the meaning of that evolution . . ."

14. "Modern youth are searching for that meaning!"

15. The celebrated scientist gave a sorrowful sigh, closed his penknife and remarked portentously: "But why, in that case, are they all so full of pretension? What an absence of honesty and nobility there is in these affectations."

16. Both of them were wrong.


1. In the tidy little study of archpriest Father Blagosklonsky, the golden-bearded prophet overflowed with complaints.

2. He had come scurrying here, pale and distraught, and Father Ioann was holding his cold hands.

3. "What *is* this, Father? What on earth *is* this? It was neither dream, nor reality."

4. "My heart bleeds, and I am burning like fire!"

5. The white priest bowed gently over the head of the terrified man. He comforted him with his deep-blue eyes, the eyes of a child.

6. Silently he smoothed his golden curls, and the ascetic's heart contorted painfully with the old man's kindness.

7. While the kind priest asked him in a whisper: "Are you very much in love with her?"

8. And he confided his perfidious dreams to the priest, like a confused child confiding in an older, virtuous one.

9. Outside the slush was melting, and the priest's face looked wrinkled and yellowish-green beneath the gloomy clouds.


1. "But what on earth *was* it yesterday? Who are they? Can such horrors genuinely happen in reality?"

2. At this point the priest hung his head very low, as if caught in a midemeanour. He seemed enveloped in a scarcely visible, misty veil.

3. At last, shaking his locks and with a despairing wave of his old hand, he said: "Don't try to delve any deeper by asking what this is."

4. "All kinds of things happen . . . But about *this* you must keep silent . . ."

5. "Do I not see that we are all flying somewhere at breakneck speed?"

6. "Do I not understand *what this* means?"

7. "Take now, for instance. Can you not see that there is something alien between us, something harmful, something terrifying?"

8. The ascetic looked at the downcast image of the old man, blurred by a misty veil. The old man reached in alarm for the crucifix round his neck.

9. The golden-bearded one looked around him and realised that *all was not as it should be.*

10. They looked at each other in silence, and Sergey Musatov whispered: *"And so it approaches . . . So it approaches from all directions!"*

11. They crossed themselves in silence, and the priest read out the words: "May God be raised again from the dead!"

12. Then Father Ioann sat Sergey Musatov down and they conversed quietly about general mysteries.

13. "Now, when you suffer misfortune and your soul burns with love, *they* are circling above you in an invisible cloud, a terrible storm-cloud, driving you into despair, unfurling the scroll of terror . . ."

14. "Love and pray! Universal love triumphs over everything!"

15. Ioann did not say much of universal love, accepting and rejecting nothing, but a white breeze blew from these words and dispersed the *terrible host.*

16. Musatov and the white priest stood together on the slushy roadway, which was enveloped in gloomy mist.

17. The priest went off to take vespers, while Musatov took a cab and went home, intending to pack his bags and travel that very evening to his brother Pavel, who was drowning in drunkenness in the country.

18. At the junction of two streets the cab-driver halted, because a funeral procession was approaching.

19. They were conducting the deceased section-head to his final resting-place.

20. God's servant, Dormidon Ivanovich, had passed away after a short, but grave illness.

21. So the funeral procession filed past, led by the hatless undertaker.

22. He held a tiny icon wrapped in a white towel.

23. Day was dying, like a mournful candle . . .

1. "I am bored . . . This life doesn't satisfy me . . ."

2. "I smile like a doll, while my soul begs for that which is not, and which might have been, but did not come about."

3. The fairy-tale burst into tears by the window and raised her perfumed handkerchief to her deep-blue eyes.

4. And the centaur hung his head and said nothing, biting his nails in mortification.

5. He had done whatever lay in his power to please the woman he loved.

145

6. And she wept by the window and whispered: "Bored, bored!" She watched mechanically as the yardmen cleared away the dirty slush in the street.

7. Outside a street-lamp was lit . . . And then a diamond star flashed in her luxuriant hair.

8. And she resembled a sacred vision.

9. Day was dying like a mournful candle.


1. A railway track stretched across the snowy plains. A train was rushing along the rails.

2. In the carriage it was cold. Musatov sat wrapped up in his fur-coat.

3. The fairy-tale kept appearing before him. She smiled sarcastically into his face with those coral-coloured lips of hers, and he whispered: "I love you."

4. On the other side of the partition, in the next compartment, two men were talking.

5. One was shouting: "You mustn't think otherwise . . . We *know* a few things, we *expect* a few things . . . We are interested in the Gospel . . ."

6. "Poppycock . . ." snorted the other.


1. The mystics' escapades had infuriated the press. Liberals, populists and former Marxist remnants had joined together and routed their handful of opponents, relying on the support of public opinion.

2. One article drew attention to itself, and its author became popular.

3. It was entitled: "Mysticism and Physiology" . . . And no mystic could be found to refute it.

4. They were too distressed about Musatov's flight from Moscow, about the fading of the new-born star.

5. Only Shipovnikov, the mystic from Saint-Petersburg, picked up the proffered gauntlet and responded with a paragraph which began and ended with the words: *"Well, so what?"*

1. New times were coming.

2. The new times brought no news. God knows why they were getting so impassioned.

3. A terrible calamity all but exploded over Moscow.

4. An old woman arrived in Moscow by goods-train. As she got down onto the platform with a basket in her hand, she stopped the chief guard and dragged a black cockerel out of the basket.

5. To the astonished guard's enquiry as to what this meant, she replied: "Last year someone had a dream: three times the royal gates in church opened and three times a cockerel walked through: a white one, a red one and a black one."

6. "The white one signified harvest, the red one — war, and the black one — sickness."

7. "We have eaten bread, we have fought with the yellow-skinned Mongol and now we shall die . . ."

8. The harmful old woman was removed from Moscow, and people forgot about the cockerel.

9. It began scurrying around Moscow, and from that point people began to sicken with plague.

10. But stringent measures put paid to the horror.


1. That evening there was a sunset. The sky was crimson . . . An aimless tenderness spread over the whole earth.

2. Standing on Voronukhin Hill was someone *quiet* and *knowing*. He had pulled up the collar of his quilted overcoat. He was wearing a peaked cap with a cockade.

3. He was looking at the factories and vegetable-gardens spread out beneath his eyes, and there was such power in his gaze and such faith in his features that all fears seemed to have faded.

4. The tip of his nose had turned slightly red with the cold, and he said: "Yes, yes, Lord! *I see Thee.*"

5. He went off to drink a cup of tea at old woman Mertvago's.

147

1. Sitting in old woman Mertvago's house was Father Ioann. There was a ring at the door.

2. She was being visited by someone neither old, nor young, but *passive and knowing*.

3. She introduced her visitor to Father Ioann, remarking affably: "And this is Aleksey Sergeyevich Petkovsky[30] . . . You've already heard about him more than once, Father."

4. And the priest laughed, and offering the visitor his ageing hands said joyfully: "We could do with more like you!"

5. All three sat at a round table at old woman Mertvago's. The samovar hissed and blew warm steam into their faces.

6. Through the window you could see the deep-blue sky darkening and slowly scattering diamond trails of stars.

7. Old woman Mertvago poured them tea, and they conversed quietly.

8. Father Ioann was saying: "This was only the first attempt . . . Their failure will not destroy us . . . We do not lack faith. We have discovered *much* and expect *much* . . . "

9. "They were not following the right path. They perished . . . We conclude nothing, we say nothing . . . We can only await Thy Glory, Lord."

10. "Now surely you can see that it is *nigh* . . . That it is already *hanging above us*. . . That there is not long to wait . . . That the unexpected approaches . . ."

11. And to this the visitor replied, as he finished his second cup of tea: "It is so, Lord! I know Thee . . ."

12. And they were silent . . . And in silence they listened to the eternal *approach* . . . And it seemed that *something was flying with sound and singing* . . .

13. And it seemed that somewhere on the other side of the wall *someone's footsteps approached* . . .

14. And old woman Mertvago was also silent. She also heard the *eternal approach* as she washed up the cups.

15. And already it was night . . . Diamond trails of stars were being scattered.

16. The Milky Way descended lower than it should. Like a white mist, it shone with past youth and dreams beyond recall.

17. And in the front garden the trees, raising their bony arms beneath the pressure of the fresh breeze, exulted and cried in a sing-song voice: "Lo! The bridegroom comes at midnight!"


1. And once again youthful spring arrived. Within the cloister the pink cathedral with its gold and white cupolas rose into the sky. All around it were marble tombstones and little shrines.

2. The trees murmured over the lonely dead.

3. This was the kingdom of frozen tears.

4. And once again, as a year before, the young apple tree flowered, spreading its white, fragrant blossom near the little red cottage.

5. These were flowers of oblivion, the oblivion of suffering and sorrows, these were flowers of the new day.

6. And again, and again the nun was seated beneath the apple-tree, convulsively fingering her rosary.

7. And again, and again the red sunset laughed as it rippled the little apple-tree with a breeze . . . .

8. And again the tree sprinkled the nun with flowers of oblivion . . .

9. The screech of stone-martins could be heard, and the nun was burning aimlessly in the glow of the sunset . . . .


1. And again, and again a beautiful young lady in spring attire wandered among the graves . . .

2. It was the fairy-tale.

3. And again, and again they looked at each other, she and the nun, smiling at each other as if they were acquainted.

4. Wordlessly they told each another that all was not yet lost, that many sacred joys yet remained for people . . .

5. *That it was coming, that it was drawing closer*, the cherished, the impossible, the pensively sad . . .

6. And the fairy-tale stood as if enchanted among the graves, listening to the sound of the metal wreaths swaying in the wind.

7. The future was revealing itself before her, and she was burning with joy . . .

8. She *knew*.

9. Here and there on the graves little flames were sending out puffs of smoke.

10. The black nun would light icon-lamps over certain graves and over others would light any.

11. The wind rattled the metal wreaths, and a clock slowly struck the hours.

12. The dew was falling on a grey stone shrine engraved with the words: "Peace be with you, Anna, my wife!"

# NOTES

1. For a discussion of the implications of the phrase "ideal-symbolical" see p. 145 of the present volume.
2. Identified by Biely in his unpublished "Material For An Intimate Biography" (1923) as Mikhail Vasil'yevich Nesterov (1862-1942), a member of the Wanderers group of painters, noted especially for his works on religious themes.
3. Arnold Böcklin (1827-1901), a Swiss "Symbolist" painter, well known for depicting mythical creatures like mermaids, centaurs and satyrs in his work.
4. A reference to Lev Tolstoy.
5. An ironic reference to Part One of Friedrich Nietzsche's *Thus Spake Zarathustra* (1883). In the first of his discourses Zarathustra names "three transformations of the spirit: how the spirit became camel, and the camel a lion, and the lion at last a child." The camel's willingness to bear great spiritual burdens, the lion's freedom to create new values, and the child's innocent ability to forget the old and say Yes to a new beginning are what lie behind Zarathustra's allegory.
6. Max Nordau (1849-1923), Hungarian physician and author of an influential book entitled *Degeneration* (1893) which claimed to prove that many works of modern art and literature had their source in the psychological degeneracy of their authors.
7. A reference to the Club de la Noblesse in Moscow where concerts of the Philharmonic Society used to take place before the Revolution.
8. Two leading poets of the Russian Symbolist movement.
9. Identified by Biely in "Material for an Intimate Biography" as Vasily Vasil'yevich Rozanov (1856-1919), critic and writer on philosophical, religious and sexual questions.
10. Vladimir Sergeyevich Solov'yov (1853-1900), Russia's most famous religious philosopher. See Introduction.
11. See note 5.
12. Two- and three-branched candlesticks held aloft by Russian Orthodox bishops when pronouncing solemn benediction.
13. I.e. Henrik Ibsen.
14. A further reference to Tolstoy.
15. I.e. Maurice Maeterlinck (1862-1949), Belgian poet and dramatist.
16. I.e. Joris-Karl Huysmans (1848-1907), French Decadent novelist who eventually arrived at Roman Catholicism by way of Satanism.
17. I.e. Oscar Wilde, according to the critic Ivanov-Razumnik in his book *Aleksandr Blok: Andrei Biely* (Petersburg, 1919, p. 55).
18. According to Ivanov-Razumnik this is probably a reference to Joséphin Péladan (1859-1918), one of the revivers of Rosicrucianism in France. When he left the order in 1890 he bestowed upon himself the title of Sâr, or magus.
19. I.e. Cesare Lombroso (1839-1909), Italian criminologist who attempted to relate criminal behaviour to the biological characteristics of its perpetrators. Max Nordau dedicated his *Degeneration* to Lombroso (See note 6).
20. I.e. Leo XIII (b. 1810, Pope from 1878 to 1903).
21. I.e. Dmitry Sergeyevich Merezhkovsky (1865-1941), Symbolist novelist and critic. Ivanov-Razumnik has suggested that Leavenovsky (Drozhzhikovsky in the original Russian) was also based on the same, "real-life" prototype, but Biely expressly refers to the former as an "invented character" in his "Material for an Intimate Biography".

22. A reference to the views of Nikolay Fyodorovich Fyodorov (1828-1903), a philosopher known to have exercised considerable influence on Dostoyevsky, Tolstoy and Solov'yov. In his teachings, published posthumously as *The Philosophy of the Common Cause* (1906 and 1913), he advanced the view that transcendent resurrection should be preceded by immanent resurrection. Science would reveal the laws governing the metamorphosis of matter and would eventually be able to reconstitute the bodily substance of individuals long dead.

23. The Sanskrit formula uttered by the sage of the hindu *Upanishads* signifying the inner identity of the individual with the world as a whole.

24. See note 9.

25. In a letter to Invanov-Razumnik of 20 November, 1915 Biely revealed that the prototype for this character has been his own former teacher, the proprietor and director of one of Moscow's best private grammar-schools, Lev Ivanovich Polivanov (1838-1899). *Lev* in Russian means "lion": *Bars* means "snow-leopard". An oblique reference, to say the least!

26. The references here are to Patanjali, the author of the *Yoga-Sutras*, and to Shri Shankarachariya, a Vedanta philosopher who affirmed that there is only one true reality (*brahman*), and eternal principle that is the source of all things. Samkhya is another of the systems of Hindu philosophy, one which affirms a dualism between matter and soul or self (*purusha*).

27. A reference to the final scene of Ibsen's final drama *When We Dead Awaken* (1899). The Moscow Arts Theatre under Konstantin Stanislavsky and Vladimir Nemirovich-Danchenko performed the play at the end of 1900.

28. A transparent reference to Fyodor Ivanovich Shalyapin (1873-1938), the great Russian bass.

29. This obscure passage has been convincingly interpreted by Vladimir Alexandrov in his book *Andrei Biely: The Major Symbolist Fiction*, Cambridge, Mass., 1985, pp. 200-1. "An echo of V. Solv'yov's attack on Tolstoy in his preface to the *Three Converstions* [1900] is heard in what one of the beings says about knocking a length of pipe into the ground and showing the emptiness inside to fools. Solov'yov has compared Tolstoy's version of Christianity to a sect he had once read about called *vertidyrniki* (hole twisters) or *dryomolyai* (hole prayers), who, if Solov'yov is to be taken seriously, bored holes in the walls of their homes and prayed into them: *izba moya, dyra moya, spasi menya* (my hut, my hole, save me). This degree of 'simplification' reminded Solov'yov of Tolstoy's modifications of Christianity..."

30. In his letter to Ivanov-Razumnik, already quoted, Biely revealed that the prototype for this recurring figure was his university friend, Aleksey Sergeyevich Petrovsky (1881-1958), or rather "one half of him: the other half becme Popovsky...At that time he was undergoing a very painful crisis as he turned from materialism and scepticism to a 'mystical' awareness which then split further: one moment he was on his way to becoming a doubting supporter of the Church', and the next a pure and lucid mystic. Since the *Symphony* was written for my friends, for an intimate circle, I decided to express my attitude to these two sides of my friend *pedagogically..."

# A NOTE ON "THE FORMS OF ART"

"The Forms of Art" was written in the summer of 1902, shortly after the appearance of the *Dramatic Symphony*, and was first published in the December 1902 issue of Dyagilev's journal *The World of Art (Mir iskusstva)*. It represents Bely's first attempt to formulate an aesthetic theory, an undertaking to which hundreds of pages were to be devoted in subsequent years. Certain of the ideas and intuitions underlying the experimental form of the *Symphony* receive a theoretical expression in the essay.

At the basis of the argument lies a classification of art forms that is openly derived from Schopenhauer. An ascending scale is posited from the forms that exist in space to those that exist in time, with the three-dimensional art of architecture at one extreme, and the one-dimensional art of music at the other. According to Schopenhauer the function of art is to express what he calls Ideas, rather than the phenomena which are their mere reflection. Bely takes over this notion loosely, justifying the assertion of a qualititative difference between art forms by the argument that the less directly the physical phenomena of reality are reproduced, the more fully their inner truth can be conveyed. Music contains no element of phenomenal representation, but provides, alone among the arts, a direct expression of the World-Will, that baneful essence of reality which crowns Schopenhauer's system.

Onto this Schopenhauerian scheme certain other lines of thought are grafted. Bely himself pointed out that the essay showed the influence of the chemist, Wilhelm Ostwald, one of the scientists whose work he was studying as part of his university course. Ostwald attempted to establish a monistic system in which everything could be accounted for in terms of the transformation of energy. Bely developed from this his own notion of the "creative energy" of the artist.[1] In "The Forms of Art" he is seen to argue that this "creative energy" is most efficiently transformed into works of art when it encounters least resistance from the material employed. This becomes another reason for preferring art forms that are less bound to the physical world. Bely returned to a consideration of the affinity between Schopenhauer and Ostwald in an essay from 1904, where he argued that a rapprochement between natural science and metaphysics was evident in the similarity between their respective notions of "will" and "energy".[2]

The third principal ingredient of the essay is its evolutionism. Not only is music the highest form of art, but all art is moving towards music. The anticipation of imminent Apocalypse which plays such an ambiguous role in the *Symphony* is expressed in "The Forms of Art" in a relatively muted form. But that, of course, is the real meaning behind the intimations of an unknown future with which the essay ends. What emerges here is not so much the belief in necessary progress that Bely could find in Herbert Spencer, as the belief in the "theurgic" function of art that he and his contemporaries derived from Vladimir Solov'yov. Art has the ultimate purpose of serving as an active force in the process of reuniting the fallen world with God, and in Bely's view it is through its gravitation towards music that this will be fulfilled..

The fact that this crucial idea was merely intimated but not properly developed was the main point that Alexander Blok made in his first letter to Bely of January 1903. The unexplained gap between "music" in the sense of an art form, subject to aesthetic description, and "music" in a metaphorical and mystical sense, was fully acknowledged in Bely's answering letter.[3] However, it was a problem that he was never ultimately to resolve, and the dual meaning of the word "music" in his theoretical writing has bedevilled critical discussion of it.

Within the realm of the aesthetic Bely nevertheless has some important things to say. He distinguishes, for instance, between the proper and improper meaning of musicality in poetic works, reserving the "proper" meaning for "the character of the words and the manner of their disposition". It is thus essentially the structural features of a work that create its affinity to music. Despite his quotation from Verlaine near the end of the essay, the merely euphonic is not the basis of Bely's comparison between linguistic art and music.[4]

Most crucially, perhaps, "The Forms of Art" constitutes an attack upon rationalism in art. In Bely's argument it follows from the fact that art is not called upon to reproduce the phenomena of the world, that the relations between its parts, the images of which it is composed, should not be seen in the same light as the relations between phenomena. The principle of coherence governing the relations between images is not necessarily logical. He envisages a poetic work in which the coherence of the imagery

156

is not explicable by reference to a coherence in the external world, but has to be perceived as entirely immanent to the work itself. When he ultimately comes to characterise it, however, he employs words which have a convenient ambiguity, touching at once upon the psychological and the musical: "nastroyenie", "nastroyennost'", meaning "mood" or "key".

This is one of a number of echoes between the preface to the *Dramatic Symphony* and "The Forms of Art". Another can be found in Bely's interpretation of Ibsen, where he speaks of the combination of the temporal and the non-temporal, the allegory that shows through an everyday drama, the suffusion of drama with the spirit of music. Just as he asserts in the preface that it is the combination of the satirical and musical with the ideal that leads to symbolism, so in the essay he argues that symbolism arises inevitably from the combination of the dramatic and the musical.

The idea of symbolism underlying these formulations is based on a traditional metaphysical dualism. Through the individual phenomena, but without cancelling them, the noumenal truth is glimpsed; the symbol is the combination of the two. However, there is already a tension between this essentially static notion and the dynamism inherent in Bely's "theurgic" or apocalyptic view of art. In later years the apparent stasis of this formulation will more and more clearly give way to a view in which art creates a new reality, rather than reflecting an eternal one.

A word is needed about the translation of the word "ideynyy" which occurs both in the preface and in the article. In modern Soviet usage this word has come to mean "possessing high ideological content", or simply "ideological". It seems clear, however, that in Bely's language it is simply the most straightforward adjective derived from the noun "idea", and means no more than "pertaining to Ideas". It relates specifically, of course, to the sense in which Schopenhauer uses the term to express the function of art. In all instances it has been translated by the most neutral English word available: "ideal".

John Elsworth

## NOTES

1. See Maria Deppermann, *Andrej Belyjs Ästhetische Theorie des Schöpferischen Bewusstseins*, Munich 1982, p. 81.
2. A. Bely, "Krititsizm i simvolism", *Simvolizm*, Moscow, 1910, p. 23. (Originally in *Vesy*, 1904, No. 2)
3. A. Blok i A Bely, *Perepiska*, Moscow, 1940, pp. 3, 8.
4. See Ada Steinberg, *Word and Music in the Novels of Andrey Bely*, Cambridge, 1982, pp. 25-6.

# THE FORMS OF ART

*Translated by Dr John Elsworth*

I

Art rests upon reality. The reproduction of reality may be either the goal of art, or its point of departure. In relation to art reality is, as it were, the food, without which its existence is impossible. All food goes to the support of life. For this its assimilation is necessary. The translation of reality into the language of art is likewise accompanied by a certain processing. This processing, while in its interior meaning a synthesis, leads to the analysis of surrounding reality. The analysis of reality follows necessarily from the impossibility of conveying by means of exterior devices the fullness and variety of all the elements of surrounding reality.

Art is not able to convey the fullness of reality, that is, mental representations and their succession in time. It dissects reality, depicting it either in spatial or in temporal forms. That is why art dwells either upon the representation, or upon the succession of representations: in the first instance spatial art forms arise, in the second — temporal ones. It is the impossibility of dealing with reality in all its fullness that gives rise to the schematisation of reality (in particular, for examination, stylisation). The power of a work of art is very often associated with simplicity of expression. Owing to such schematisation the creator of a work of art has the possibility of expressing himself, albeit less fully, more exactly, more distinctly.

The reproduction of a mental representation independently of time is accompanied by immense difficulties. On the one hand there is the difficulty of conveying various spatial forms; on the other, that of conveying all the imaginable nuances of light and colour with the help of exterior means. If we add to this fact that the possibility of encompassing phenomena in an artistic depiction depends upon simplicity, then we can understand the need for the further dissection of spatial reality into its forms and colours.

In forms we are not restricted to considering the relationship of light and shade. Our attention is held both by colour, and by the quality of the form, that is to say, its material. The colour of a form is the link that

161

connects the plastic arts with painting; the material of the form compels us to stress the possibility of the existence of a further art form, the art, so to speak, of material. The quality of a material, its character, can be the object of art. Here, we find ourselves at the very limit of the fine arts. Here we become aware of two roots, that go from fine art to science and to the art industry. Here begins a consequent broadening of the very concept of art; it appears to us more and more as the artful (the artificial). Here too the profundity and sublimity of the tasks of art disappear.

Having stressed the importance of the quality of materials in the plastic arts, let us turn to the classification of their forms. If we characterise one type as the art of organic forms, and the other as that of inorganic forms we shall not be particularly far from the truth, calling sculpture the art of organic forms, and architecture that of inorganic forms.

Such a definition of architecture and sculpture appears paradoxical. For example, do we not have in the column a striving to depict the trunk of a tree? If indeed a type of column did arise from the imitation of a tree-trunk, that imitation is so external and formal (non-intrinsic), that we need not dwell upon it. The sole permanent theme of architecture, according to Schopenhauer, is support and weight.

> "Columns and beams are the purest expression of this theme. That is why the style of columns represents as it were the figured base of all architecture."

Schopenhauer points further to the aesthetic delight derived from the normality of the relations between weight and support. It is clear from this that the column depicts above all the idea of normal support, and only subsequently is it an imitation of a trunk.

In this way we have arrived at the recognition of three spatial forms of art, namely: painting, sculpture, architecture.

Colour is characteristic of painting. Material and form are characteristic of sculpture and architecture. It does not follow from this, of course, that outline and form are neglected in painting, or colour in architecture and sculpture. The succession of representations is a fact of life. The temporal forms of art, dwelling predominantly upon this succession, indicate the importance of movement. Hence the role of rhythm, as the character of temporal sequence in music, the art of pure movement. If music is the art of causeless, unconditional movement, then in poetry this movement is conditioned, limited, causal. More correctly, poetry is a bridge thrown across from space to time. Here the transition, as it were, is performed from the spatial to the temporal. In certain poetic genres this transitional character is especially clearly expressed; these genres are the central, nodal genres (drama, for example). It is this centrality of their position that gives rise to the especial interest in them. This is the source of their intimate connection with the spiritual development of humanity.

Thus, poetry is the nodal form that links time and space. According to Schopenhauer, the combination of space and time is the essence of matter. Schopenhauer defines it as causality in action. Hence the necessity of causality and motivation in poetry, as forms of "the principle of sufficient reason". This causality can be variously expressed: both by conscious clarity, accompanying the images, and by the inner groundedness of the poetic images. Logical consistency, to express the matter figuratively, is as it were the projection of caauality onto the plane of our consciousness, if we understand by consciousness what Schopenhauer defines as rational knowledge: "to know means to have in one's spirit for voluntary use judgements, which possess, in something exterior to themselves, a sufficient reason of knowing".

Poetic images, in that they stimulate our consciousness, are accompanied by consciousness more than all other forms of art. This is the key to some important misunderstandings in the sphere of the critical evaluation of artistic images. These misunderstandings are revealed in all their force as soon as we place the demand for rational clarity in this projection of causality at the forefront of the other demands which the images of poetry have to satisfy. Here a phenomenon takes place which is analogous to consonance: the vibration of one string, while conveyed by the atmosphere to other strings of identical pitch, is not conveyed to strings at other pitches. The internal coherence that connects a series of poetic images is frequently accompanied by an external coherence, that is to say, by the expression of a conscious link existing between these images viewed as a reflection of reality. It cannot be inferred from this that conscious clarity is a necessary condition of poetic creation. However, this inference is widely made. "Consciousness", in Schopenhauer's words, "is only the surface of our spirit, in which we do not know the inner kernel;" and further:- "that which gives unity and coherence to consciousness cannot be conditional upon consciousness." The demand for conscious coherence in poetic works arises from the confusion of two forms of the principle of sufficient reason, forms defined by Schopenhauer as the principle of sufficient reason of knowing, which is predominant in the class of abstract representations, and the principle of sufficient reason of being, which is applicable to the class of concrete phenomena. Creation directs consciousness, not consciousness creation.

In rationalistic works of art, as Goethe has it, "you feel the intention and become disturbed . . ." *Kunst* is derived from the word *können* (to be able): "he who can't, intends." "If we see, through all the rich devices of art, a clear, limited, cold and sober concept, which finally emerges into the light of day, we experience revulsion and disgust." "A work of art causes rapture and delight by virtue of that part of it which is not accessible to conscious comprehension; that is what the immense effect of the beautiful in art depends upon, not the parts that we are perfectly able to analyse" (Helmoltz).[1]

According to Hartmann[2] the creative thought of genius grasps the whole in an instant; conscious combination creates unity through the difficult process of adjusting particulars.

I cite with particular pleasure the words of a great scholar, two eminent philosophers and a famous music critic. Theoretically very many agree about the independence of artistic creation from the consciousness. In practice the opposite is revealed: the recognition of the freedom of creation is simply replaced by the acceptance of poetic conversations on the subject.

> "You are a Tsar — live alone: walk that free path on which your free sprit leads you."[3]

We accept these words about poetic freedom, but we are afraid to recognise any poetic passage where this creative freedom is realised (in Fet, for example). In this instinctive fear of creative freedom is expressed the powerlessness of the crowd to distinguish genius from madness; waywardness of thought is not distinguished from soaring flight, the myopic are capable of calling clarity of vision a hallucination. It is always safer to mock . . .

One of the typical features of poetry is the fact that what it depicts is indirect. In other arts we either contemplate spatial forms, or we listen to, that is to say, contemplate the sequential alternation of sounds. In either instance our contemplation is direct. In poetry we re-create, on the basis of what we read, the images and their succession. The accuracy of our contemplation will depend on the accuracy with which our consciousness re-creates the images and phenomena described. Poetry is all-embracing, but is not direct. Here the river-bed of art, which starts at architecture, floods out, as it were, into a broad lake, but grows shallow, breaks up into a multitutde of branches until by way of drama and opera it is concentrated into the pure deep channel of symphonic music.

The expression of ideas is the task of art, according to Schopenhauer; however he contrasts music with all other arts, saying that it expresses the Will, i.e. the essence of things. To comprehend a phenomenon *an sich* — means to listen to its music, that is to say, it is here that we come closest to the possibility of such comprehension.

Space has three dimensions, time — one. In the transition from the spatial forms of art to the temporal (to music) we can observe a strict gradation. The same gradation exists in the tendency of sciences towards the adoption of a mathematical (arithmological) point of view. According to Schopenhauer a parallel can be drawn between these tendencies in the sciences and the arts. Music is the mathematics of the soul, and mathematics the music of the mind. Nowhere do we encounter simultaneously such affinity and contrast as exists between the comprehension of phenomena (music) and the study of similarity and dissimilarity in the realm of their quantitative change (mathematics). "Our consciousness has as its form not space, but only time," says Schopenhauer. The world is dominated by movement, which has as its cognitive form time, and a representation is a momentary photograph of this uninterrupted succession of phenomena, this eternal movement. Any spatial image, as it becomes accessible to our consciousness, is necessarily associated with time; the law of cognition has as its basis the law of causality, which, according to Schopenhauer, is a combination of space and time. The importance of causality, which explains the visible world (the spatial), increases in proportion to the proximity of the spatial forms of art to the temporal form. The requirement of casuality in spatial images already intimates to us their connection with music; were there no music, necessarily connected with time through the succession of sonar vibrations, in the forms that are subordinate to space, we would not be able to detect the causality of these images. This is the genesis of the idea that music influences all forms of art but is at the same time independent of them. To anticipate, let us say that every form of art has reality for its point of departure, and music, as pure movement, for its destination.

To express ourselves in Kantian language — all art, proceeding from the phenomenal, penetrates into the "noumenal"; to formulate our thought in the language of Schopenhauer, — all art leads us to the pure contemplation of the World-Will; or, to speak in the spirit of Nietzsche, — every form of art is determined by the degree to which the spirit of music is revealed in it; or, according to Spencer,[4] — all art tends towards the future.

The universal significance of this last formula is extremely important in the examination of art from the point of view of religious symbolism.

If we place the fine arts in their order of perfection we arrive at the following five principal forms: architecture, sculpture, painting, poetry, music.

No form of art is entirely self-contained. Elements inherent in all forms are capriciously intertwined in each particular form. As they emerge into the foreground they form as it were the centre of the form in question. Thus, although we regard colour as central to painting, nevertheless painting without form or without meaning (i.e. lacking external meaning) is possible only to a certain extent in the ornament. On the one hand, the ornament gains nothing from any meaning attributed to it, for the ornament will express the individuality of the race even without that meaning. On the other hand, it is unthinkable to demand of painting nothing but an ornamental quality. In historical painting, genre painting or religious painting what holds our attention is the *meaning* of what is depicted. Here also, we turn our attention to form as well. The meaningfulness, the spirituality of Raphael, Giotto, Sandro-Botticelli is clear to us, but we take delight in the forms of Michelangelo. Causality, motivation are the principal elements of poetry; the causal element in painting brings it closer to poetry — a more perfect art.

Beauty and precision of form are the link which connects painting with the less perfect plastic arts, the arts of physical form. In poetry we observe elements typical of both the spatial and the temporal forms: both representations and their succession, a combination of the physical with the musical. Besides the musicality of poetic works in an improper sense, it is possible to speak of their musicality in a proper sense. In the character of the words and the manner of their disposition we perceive a greater or lesser musicality. The immediate attitude of an author to his own poetic images can often be sensed in the character of the words and the manner of their disposition. The style of a poet or writer is the non-verbal accompaniment to the verbal expression of the poetic images. A profound writer cannot possess a bad style. A bad writer has not style. Style, as musical accompaniment, has to play a prominent role. In oral performance the significance of the musicality of poetic images increases; many passages of Homer and Virgil beg to be spoken out loud. In the song the musical meaning takes precedence over the physical meaning. *How* it is sung is more important to us than *what* is sung. The song is a bridge between poetry and music. Both poetry and music grew out of the song.

"From a historical point of view music developed out of the song", says

Helmholtz in his work *Die Lehre von den Tonempfindungen*. The folk-song, in Nietzsche's words, "has meaning for us above all as a musical mirror of the world, as an original melody which then seeks for itself a parallel dream (i.e. image) and expresses it in verse. In this way we see that in verse the folk-song strives with all its might to imitate music." We can assume the character of musical development and the further differentiation of music from songs through the development of accompaniment; this is where the various forms of music have their beginning. The integration of these forms was accomplished relatively recently in the symphony and the sonata (a symphony for one instrument). All forms of poetry, epic, lyric and dramatic, arose from the development of the words of songs. In the dithyrambs in honour of Dionysus we have the seed of what was to become drama and opera. At the present moment drama is tending more and more towards music (Ibsen, Maeterlinck and others), and the opera towards the musical drama, and to a significant degree this tendency has been realised (Wagner).

One indubitable consequence follows from what has been said above: the forms of art are capable to some extent of merging one with another, of becoming imbued with the spirit of adjacent forms. Elements of a more perfect form, penetrating into a less perfect form, imbue it with spiritual quality, and the reverse is also true. For example, the exclusive painterliness of the poems of Sully Prudhomme or José-Maria de Heredia gives them a coldness: the exclusive tendency to the depiction of form in painting criticised by Ruskin. It is interesting that ancient culture did not produce any luxurious flowering of painting, while Christian culture did. With the spread of Christianity the centre of gravity in the spatial arts is transferred to the more perfect form: with the spread of Christianity the most sublime art — music — becomes completely free of poetry and acquires independence and development. At the present moment the human spirit is at a watershed. Beyond that watershed there begins an increased gravitation towards religious questions. Is not the pre-eminent growth of music up to Beethoven and the broadening of its sphere of influence from Beethoven to Wagner the arch-image of such a watershed?

Let us formulate two probable consequences that suggest themselves from what has been said:

First, the formal elements of each art consist of the formal elements of the adjacent art forms.

Second, the renascence of each form of art depends upon the action upon it of a more perfect form; the reverse action of it upon the other form leads to the decline of the other.

It does not, however, follow from this that the less perfect forms of the fine arts arise first: all arts are potentially contained in the song. It is from there that infinite differentiation began. The progress of painting, of sculpture and architecture was dependent not only on the psychic development of mankind, but also on the development of technical means.

It is characteristic that every higher art contains in itself all lower art forms, translated into its own language. The art of material masses is contained in painting in the sense that, while able to convey material masses on a surface, it combines with that also the possibility of conveying their colour. Poetry, by including in itself the depiction of all reality, contains the spatial forms too. Music, as we shall see below, embraces all possible combinations of reality.

It has to be noted that at the present moment all the principal forms of art are already defined. Their further development is connected with the art that stands at their head, that is to say, with music, which casts its imprint with ever increasing dominance on all the fine arts. At the present time music and the musical drama are developing swiftly and powerfully. An involuntary thought arises about the further character of the influence of music upon art. Will not all forms of the fine arts seek more and more to occupy the place of the overtones in relation to the basic tone, i.e. to music?

But the future is unknown . . . .

II

In every form of art its aesthetic meaning can be perceived. By a form of art we mean a set of methods for the expression of the beautiful, which are connected with each other by a certain unity in their external manifestation.

For many types of poetry this unity is the word, for painting it is colours, for music — sound, for sculpture and architecture — material. It is possible to speak of the quality and the quantity of material necessary for the form.

It is important that the smallest quantity of material for the form should be applied in the best way possible to the expression of the content. The full communication of artistic content depends not only on the quantity of material, but also on its quality. Laconic brevity is an essential feature of art: it is better to understate than to overstate. Form and content stand in an inverse relationship to each other.

Artistic content, bound by form, appears to us in the shell of concrete images and their succession. Certain forms of art provide the possibility of cognising that artistic content by means of a small quantity of material representations: they meet most satisfactorily the purpose of art.

Let us examine from this point of view the principal forms of fine art. What conclusions emerge from such an examination?

In the least perfect forms of art the formal reproduction of reality is at its fullest. These forms are architecture and sculpture. In reality every image occupies a position defined by three dimensions; in sculpture and architecture artistic images cannot be embodied otherwise than in three dimensions. Fundamental examination of these forms necessarily leads to the recognition that they encompass reality in the most one-sided way. Partly omitting the variety of colour in the images of reality, and also their succession, the plastic arts narrow down the very selection of these images. Only certain real images can serve as the objects of depiction, and even then in their abstract conventional form.

In painting we have to do with the projection of reality onto a plane. In depicting on a plane spatial forms measurable by height, length and width, we make the transition from three dimensions to two. Here we have to do with an external idealisation or reality; this idealisation, however, allows us to depict a wider range of reality; this is not accessible to architecture and sculpture. The transfer of a spatial representation onto a plane liberates us to a substantial extent from purely physical labour; such labour is a necessary condition in the creation of architectural and sculptural monuments. The inner energy, undistracted by external impediments, is conveyed in fuller measure to a picture or fresco: among works of the brush we have excellent examples of how to communicate the subtlest emotional aspects of reality. It is as though, by renouncing one dimension, we acquire the possibility of additionally encompassing reality from the aspect of colour as well. The depiction of reality in colour is the most typical feature of painting. In sculpture the forms of reality depicted by means of material substances often present an interest to us from the point of view of the play of light and shade. In painting we are interested also in the colour aspect of reality.

In the arts it is important that the smallest quantity of material should express as fully as possible the content that the artist seeks to put into it. A consistent examination of the quantity and quality of material required for the embodiment of an artistic idea in architecture, sculpture and painting leads us to the following conclusion: of the spatial forms of art painting is the most perfect form; sculpture occupies a place between it and architecture.

And indeed, with the aid of a small quantity of colours we attain the fullest depiction on canvas not only of a single image or group of images, but of whole events. Architecture and sculpture are unable to depict large spaces: in painting such depiction is possible (landscape, for instance). The reduction of external impediments stands as it were in a direct relationship with freedom of creation. The inner energy, since it is not being expended on the overcoming of these impediments, is conveyed more fully into the embodied image. This image is able to possess a greater potential power. Slavish copying of reality cannot lead to an identity between the depiction and the object of depiction. The inner truth of the object conveyed is the principal object of depiction. It is not the picture itself that has to stand in the foreground, but the truthfulness of the feelings and moods experienced, and evoked in us by any given painting of nature. Such an understanding of the tasks of the depiction of reality stems by no means from a feeling of disdain for reality, but from a feeling of profound love of nature. The question of truth in nature is much more complex and confused than appears at first sight.

The inner truth of what is depicted may be understood variously. One and the same picture, depicted by many artists, will be refracted, in Zola's expression, through the prism of their souls. Each artist will see different aspects of it. Therefore individualism is to some extent essential in painting; artists are individual, as are artistic schools. Each school may give us both talented artists and untalented ones. The question of the tasks of painting is not a matter of artistic schools. It stands above all schools. The question of beauty is not a matter of tendencies in painting either. Beauty is various and the sense of beauty is much more complex than many people think.

> "Beautiful objects remain beautiful wthout having any features at all in common except that we find them beautiful. This is the judgement on such theories (i.e. theories that seek an over-hasty unification of beauty) made by Stewart."

So says Troitsky in his work *German Psychology in the Present Century.*[5] Painting is not a trade. It is not photography. Painting is distinguished from coloured photography, oleography and so on by the individual understanding of the inner truth of what is depicted. The attitude to nature of people who have devoted their lives to the study of its various nuances of light and hue, and of people who once in a blue moon honour it with their attention, do not always concide; conversational speech does not coincide with scientific or philosophical speech.

However, we reject out of hand forms of art which have not yet become comprehensible to us. Can there not be a certain kind of philosophy here? Can there not be works of art that demand on our part a certain effort of penetration into their meaning? Does not the depth of artistic contemplation put a certain stamp on the depiction of that which is contemplated? Is it possible that a layman in painting who has turned up at an exhibition to make fun of Vrubel'[6] or Gallen[7] has really penetrated the depth of the artistic works by such as Botticelli, Rembrandt and the like? In his heart of hearts, of course, he prefers the ethnographical sketches of Vereshchagin,[8] painted for him in a lively and accurate way (sketches that are good for the intellect); Raphael, Rembrandt, Velasquez, all these are half-decayed banners, objects of respect, with which he naively arms himself as he declares war on the new art. He does not suspect that it is the new art which represents the genuine renewal of ancient traditions in painting. He takes the revolt by some art forms against academicism and naturalism for a revolt against everything old . . . *Sancta simplicitas!*

In the plastic arts we depicted reality in three dimensions. In making the transition to the depiction of reality in only two dimensions, we gained in the quality and quantity of what is depicted; this gain facilitated the transference of the inner energy of creation into the embodied image. Assuming a priori a further regular progression we may think that in poetry we move to the depiction of reality in only one dimension (in time).

Two-dimensional space is characterised by the plane, one-dimensional — by the line. The direct communication of an image is still possible on a plane. The communication of that image on a line is not possible. If we did not know the character of the form of art which has the name poetry, we would be able a priori to predict that the depiction of poetic images is indirect.

The direct depiction of the visible world is absent in poetry. It is replaced by the verbal depiction of it. The combination of words, extended in a single line, symbolises the one-dimensionality of poetry. It is easier to describe than to depict. Owing to the replacement of depicted images by description, the range of images that can be the object of poetic reproduction is significantly increased.

The work of the sculptor is substantially paralysed by the narrow limits of depiction. The painter has greater freedom of creation; all the same many images are incommunicable with the brush (for example, the starry sky, a picture of night and so on). Such descriptions are accessible to poetry.

The inner energy of the poet comes up against external impediments even less. The sculptor uses a substantial amount of material; this material restricts his creative freedom. The painter uses a smaller amount of material (canvas and paints, applied with a brush). The poet uses hardly any at all. Nevertheless to him is given the possibility of describing the great image of reality. He is not confined by space. Painting only comes to terms with space to a certain extent.

The measurement of a line is performed by means of the successive placing upon it of another shorter line, taken as a unit. Counting plays an important part in measurement. The succession of moments in time, which conditions the process of counting, is the basis of all measurement. The immediate measurement of any reading is seen in the clearest relief in one-dimensional space — in the line. In three-dimensional space, however, the projected co-ordinate axes precede measurement. Measurement, i.e. the translation of spatial relations into temporal ones, occurs later. The line does not require definition for height or depth, only for length. We measure a line at once; we translate it at once into the language of time. Time is the simplest form of the principle of sufficient reason. The line is the symbol of one-dimensional space. One-dimensional space is the symbol of poetry; one-dimensional space is connected with time. From this we deduce a priori the proximity of poetry, a purely temporal form, to music. From this we infer the importance of movement in poetry.

And indeed, the possibility of depicting the succession of mental representations is an essential feature of poetry. Representation is impossible without space. The succession of representations presupposes time. Poetry, in depicting both representations and the succession of them, is the nodal form of art that links time with space. Causality, according to Schopenhauer, is the link between time and space. Causality has great importance in poetry. In this sense it is not this or that feature of reality that is the object of depiction in poetry, but all reality. All the advantage of poetry over painting, sculpture and architecture is contained in this breadth of depiction; the elements of time come to the fore, while spatial images, though lacking immediacy, are still there to be perceived. We witness a loss in the brightness of spatial images as the significance grows of their temporal succession. It is here that the analogy first suggests itself between this conversion of form and the conversion of energy. In the given instance poetry plays the role of a spatial equivalent of music, analogous, for example, with the mechanical equivalent of heat. Poetry is the vent that lets the spirit of music into the spatial forms of art. "It bloweth where it listeth, and thou hearest the sound thereof, but canst not tell whence it cometh, and whither it goeth" (St. John). Here we have a hint of an impulse of a single kind that is given to all forms of art; the difference in the tasks of these forms follows from their different qualities. When we put a burning match consecutively for a specific period of time to a pound of stone, a pound of wood, a pound of cotton-wool and a pound of gun-powder, we get different effects; the stone becomes slightly warm, while the powder explodes, developing a mass of energy, — although the source of heat was the same.

Poetry, in connecting time with space, brings into the foreground the law of causality and motivation. The centre of poetry lies not in form and not in colour, but in the causal succession of these colours and forms, combined together into images of surrounding reality. Let us remember the words of Schopenhauer: "The subjective correlative of matter or causality, since both are the same, — is the understanding (*Verstand*)." Kant called the subjective correlative of time and space pure sense. The understanding is manifested, according to Schopenhauer, in contemplation of the world. That which is directly comprehended by the understanding is linked by the reason (*Vernunft*) into concepts; further combinations of these concepts give birth to a series of inferences. Poetry has to do with the understanding in Schopenhauer's sense, but is by no means rational. The presence of rationality in poetry has to be regarded as a certain kind of mutuality, existing between that which is contemplated and those who contemplate it. This mutuality is particularly strong in certain forms of poetry, which depict the social and intellectual life of individual people or whole nations, as we see in the novel. These forms of poetry are greatly developed; their particular purpose obscures the principal aim of art. This is the origin of the colossal mistake of proclaiming *tendentiousness* to be the principal aim of art.

The principle of art for art's sake, which is in the air, was able to have a temporary significance as one extreme balancing the opposite extreme. Real artists took their stance under this banner; this arose from an unclear awareness of the real principle of art. Both tendentiousness and the absence of it are separate aspects, determined by a higher principle.

There remains one essential question in poetry for us to clarify. How is it that rationality has imposed its stamp upon poetry and extended from there into the other arts?

Schopenhauer dwells upon the confusion between two forms of the principle of sufficient reason. "That form of the principle of sufficient reason, which relates only to concepts or abstract ideas, is transferred to concrete ideas, real objects, and demands a sufficient reason of knowing from objects which can only possess a sufficient reason of being. The principle of sufficient reason governs abstract ideas in the sense that each of them derives its value, its meaning and its whole existence, in that event called truth, solely and exclusively from the relationship of the judgement to something situated outside itself, to the sufficient reason of knowing. The principle of sufficient reason governs real objects, concrete ideas, on the other hand, not as a law of sufficient reason of knowing but only of being, as causality. Therefore the demand for sufficient reason of knowing in this instance has neither sense nor meaning, since it relates to a completely different class of objects".

The poetic depiction of reality is subject to the law of causality and motivation. The scientific study of reality is subject to the principle of sufficient reason of knowing. The succession of poetic images may or may not be accompanied by an awareness of their logical groundedness. A given succession of images may also exist on the basis of a groundedness that is not logical.

However, the meaningfulness of poetic images is often defined by the presence of a logical groundedness. This fatal error brings confusion into judgements about the virtues of poetic works.

In many instances our life takes such a form that its rational aspect is placed in the foreground. That is the reason why we are prepared to regard all manifestations of life through the prism of the principle of sufficient reason of knowing. We forget that the realm of art is outside the competence of this principle. We are always ready to foist upon art features that do not belong to it, or to reject achievements in the fine arts. In the first instance art appears to us as something shallow and non-essential; in the second it frightens us. We look upon manifestations of art as something senseless, irrational, almost insane, when it is, so to speak, supra-rational. When confronted with art we often resemble blind people without a guide, when the laws of logic, for all their completeness, do not explain anything to us in the realm of the emotions experienced.

Art is neither logical nor illogical, it is ideal. This ideality includes both the concept of logicality and the concept of illogicality. Ideality is the sole essential principle of art. Without cutting across formal principles, it is the more central interpretation of them.

The direct communication of one or another aspect of reality — such is the realm of the spatial forms of art. In poetry we have encountered the indirect communication of the whole of reality. In the most typical forms of music visible reality disappears . . .

"If it is asked what is expressed by the material of sounds, one has to answer: musical ideas," says Hanslick.[9]

The most typical forms of music are image-less. Music is not concerned with the depiction of forms in space. It is, as it were, outside space.

Reality is not how it appears to us. Whether we maintain a scientific, a philosophical or a religious point of view, we shall come to the same result. Reality as we know it is different from reality as it truly is.

Any attentive contemplation of the images of reality brings us to the conviction that they do not remain unchanged. Movement is the basic feature of reality. It governs images. It creates those images. They are conditioned by movement.

The world of reality that surrounds us is a deceptive picture which we have created. In the proper sense there are no representations, that is to say, there are no two moments of time in which some change does not come about in a representation, even if we were not to notice it. Only movement exists. A representation is a momentary photograph; the succession of representations is a series of such photographs, conditioned by beginning and end. To speak in the language of the Hindus, between the world and us is extended the deceptive veil of Maia.

In all religions there exists a contrast between one world and another, better one.

In the arts we have a similar contrast between spatial and temporal forms. Architecture, sculpture and painting are concerned with the images of reality, music — with the inner aspect of those languages, i.e. with the movement that governs them. This is what Hanslick says: "The beauty of a musical piece is a specifically musical beauty, i.e. consisting in the combinations of sounds without any relation to that which is foreign to them, the extra-musical sphere of ideas. The realm of music is indeed not of this world."

Starting from the lower forms of art and finishing with music, we witness a slow but sure weakening of the images of reality. In architecture, sculpture and painting these images play an important part. In music they are absent. As it approaches music a work of art becomes both deeper and broader.

I consider it necessary to repeat the words I said above: every form of art has reality for its point of departure and music, as pure movement, for its destination. Or, to express it in Kantian language, all art penetrates into the "noumenal." Or, according to Schopenhauer, all art leads us to pure contemplation of the World-Will. Or, speaking the language of Nietzsche, every form of art is defined by the degree to which the spirit of music is revealed in it. Or, as Spencer has it, all art tends towards the future. Or, finally, "the realm of music is indeed not of this world."

At the present moment the human spirit is at a watershed.

Beyond that watershed begins an increased gravitation towards religious questions. Music is exercising a stronger and stronger influence upon all forms of art. Music is about the future.

"He that hath an ear, let him hear . . ."

In an examination of art from the point of view of content the significance of music is underlined as an art which reflects the noumenal world.

As an art form that expresses new forms of spiritual life, music holds our attention in an examination of art from the viewpoint of the present day and of religion.

In my essay the formal dependence of the arts one on another and their sequence are placed in the foreground. Music, as pure movement, is the corner-stone of my conception.

In music the essence of movement is apprehended; in all infinite worlds this essence is one and the same. It is music that expresses the unity which links all these worlds, those that have been, those that are, and those that have yet to be in the future. The infinite process of perfection is gradually bringing us closer to a conscious understanding of that essence. We have to hope that it will be possible for us to come close to such an understanding in the future. In music we listen unconsciously to that essence. In music we can catch hints of a future perfection. That is why we say it is about the future. In the Revelation of St. John we have prophetic images that depict the fates of the world. "For the trumpet shall sound, and the dead shall arise, and we shall change . . .".[10] The Archangel's trump — this apocalyptic music — will it not awaken us to a final understanding of the phenomena of the world?

Music is about the future.

Music conquers the starry spaces and, in part, time. The creative energy of the poet dwells upon the choice of images for the embodiment of his ideas. The creative energy of the composer is free of that choice.

That is why music is so capable of transporting us. The heights of music rise above the heights of poetry.

In all arts our attention is held by specific images or a specificity in their succession. In music what is important is the specificity of moods. It is the specificity in the combination of sounds that holds our attention in music, and not the images or events to which it is possible with some exercise of the imagination to attribute them. A specific mood evokes in A the idea of a series of events of similar mood; B imagines a group of people, combined by a common action; C recollects a picture of nature, and so on.

If these people were to put together the programme of a musical piece, our attention would be claimed by the non-coincidence of their understanding of the meaning of a given motif. This coincidence however, would have nothing to do with the motif in question. The emotion evoked by the motif would not change from the variety of interpretations of it. Certain images and events might play the role of a bridge between life and music. They could not be the purpose of the motif. In music this or that emotion is not obscured: it has a universal character. It stands face to face with us. Embodied in other arts, it is individuated.

In the other arts the artistic images are the bearers of emotions. They are artistic to the extent that they affect our soul. As we contemplate these images we are suffused with their mood.

In music, on the contrary, images are absent. Instead of them we have to do with a motif which evokes analogous moods . . .

The awareness of an analogy between a motif and a certain image is a secondary phenomenon. In such a case we have to do with something like a deductive inference, the minor premise of which is occupied by the given image. That which is communicated indirectly in the other arts is communicated directly in music.

Hanslick has the following to say about this:

"Contemporary musical compositions, in which the dominant rhythm is interrupted by certain mysterious additions or by contrasts heaped together, are praised on the grounds that in them music, it is alleged, breaks its narrow bounds, rising to the expressiveness of speech. This praise has always seemed to us ambiguous: the bounds of music are not at all narrow, but they are very sharply delimited. Music can never rise to the level of speech — one ought to say fall, if the matter is looked at from the musical point of view — since music is clearly a far more sublime language than speech."

177

The immediately uncaused sequence of sounds is fully grounded, since time — the simplest form of the principle of sufficient reason — is the sole necessary condition of music.

A musical motif combines various pictures of analogous mood; it contains as it were an extract of all that is significant in those pictures. The language of music is a language that unites.

There exists a complete parallelism between each art, on the one hand, and particular formal features in music, on the other.

The causal succession of images is replaced by the rhythm of different tones. The seven octaves of the European scale correspond to the seven colours of the spectrum. The quality of material corresponds to pitch. The quantity corresponds to volume and so on. All arts encounter analogous features in music, but the language of music unites and generalises art.

Do not the profundity and intensity of musical works give us a hint that here the deceptive veil is removed from the visible world? In music the secrets of movement are opened up to us, the essence of movement that governs the world.

We have to do with entire universe; in poetry this universe was expressed by means of the description of the phenomena of reality; in painting — by the depiction of its colour aspect and so on. We understand the contrast between music and all the other arts that Schopenhauer and Nietzsche emphasize. We also understand the ever increasing transference of the centre of art from poetry to music. This transference takes place in proportion to the growth of our culture. We understand, finally, Verlaine's half-conscious exclamation

"De la musique avant toute chose
De la musique avant et toujours . . ."

In symphonic music the processing of reality is brought to completion; there is nowhere further to go. And yet it is in symphonies that all the power and depth of music are unfolded for the first time.

Symphonic music has developed in the recent past. We have here the last word in art. In symphonic music, the most perfect form, the tasks of art are crystallized with the greatest clarity. Symphonic music is a banner that shows the way to art in general and determines the character of its evolution.

Symphonic music is not concerned with phenomenal reality. Images in music are the product of reflection.

The demand for explanation in music has given birth to an entire school of thought; the occasional successful work written in the style of that school does not redeem its erroneousness.

The centre of music is, as before, in the symphony. This striving to explain music is evidence of a mistake analogous to the mistake indicated above in poetry.

The profundity of music and the absence of external reality in it invite the idea of the emblematic character of music as that which explains the secret of movement, the secret of being.

> Out of brief allusions,
> Depths of life revealing,
> Silently ascended
> The fateful secret.          (Vl. Solov'yov)

> Past moments with silent footfall
> Came up and suddenly lifted the veil from my eyes.
> They see something eternal, something inseparable.
> And past years like a single hour.      (Vl. Solov'yov)[11]

Here art is striving towards the same goal as science, but from the other side, the opposite and reverse. Solidarity of art with science must therefore not consist in a confusion of purpose, not in an external equation of art with scientific aims, nor in a confusion of their paths, but in a definite boundary between science and art. This boundary conditions the contrast between science and art. This contrast accustoms us to the thought that there are a variety of ways leading us to knowledge of the universe.

It follows from the foregoing that the worth of an art form that strives by means of images to convey the image-less immediacy of music is determined by its closeness to music. Every branch of art strives to express in images something typical, eternal, independent of place and time. It is in music that these vibrations of eternity are most successfully expressed. Various combinations of images and events can be attributed to them subsequently. Every particular combination is related to its musical prototype as a specific concept to a generic concept.

In the sphere of logical thought the extent and the content of a concept are in an inverse relationship. In the sphere of artistic contemplation breadth (extent) and depth (content) are as it were directly proportional. In music we have combinations of all possible realities. The extent of music is unlimited. Its content is the profoundest content. Music is not rational, but its realm is not feelings alone.

Some thinkers do not class ideas as concepts. They do not consider them to be real essences. In ideas, in their opinion, elements are contained both of the abstract and of the concrete.

The worth of a work of art cannot be determined either by its intellectual quality or by its emotional quality.

In a work of art both are present. We look at a phenomenon without making any inferences in relation to it. In these artistic reproductions of phenomena we detect something eternal. Is not this element of the eternal, independently of external circumstances, the element which has caused certain thinkers to single it out as the element of ideality? It is from this that a faint presentiment, as it were, is first born in us that the essence of art lies in its ideality. This enables us to understand the meaning of an expression that artists frequently use: they say it is not enough to see objects, one has to "know how to see". Knowing how to see is the ability to understand in images their eternal meaning, their idea. Is this not where "the music of the spheres" belongs? An examination of the ideality of art is not, however, part of our present undertaking.

We are examining art from the point of view of form. We touch upon the ideality of art only because of the dependence that exists between the discussion of art from the viewpoints of form and content.

In music this dependence is seen with particular clarity. This also is the origin of the idea of artistic creation as a synthesis of intellect and feeling, creating something else, which conditions both. The duality that exists between intellect and feeling disappears in the contemplation of artistic images. Here feeling, in the words of Geibel,[12] becomes "a calm and transparent river-bed, over which, rising and falling, there runs a torrent of sounds".

The notion of the ideality of art corresponds perfectly to this notion, which arises from the inadequacy of either rationality or emotionality by itself in art.

In every work of art our attention is held both by the image and by that which makes the image artistic. In *The Birth of Tragedy from the Spirit of Music* Nietzsche dwells upon the above-mentioned contrast in art, the contrast between the spirit of Apollo and of Dionysus. In tragedy he sees the reconciliation of these disparate principles. He foretells the progress of Dionysus from India. This is a hint of the ever-increasing penetration of music into contemporary drama. This penetration, in our profound conviction, is not limited to drama. It extends into all arts. A detailed examination of this influence would belong to the examination of art from the point of view of the present time. The expression "mood", so fashionable nowadays, has long since lost all meaning. The same thing has happened as with stolen clothes, which are, however, out of season. No-one knows what to apply the word "mood" to — it is like a label left over from the object to which it was attached. And yet the expression "mood" possesses a profound meaning. It indicates the evolution of art in the direction of music. The mood of this or that image has to be understood as the "temper" of the image, its "musical key", as it were. As we delve into the symbolic dramas of Ibsen, dramas with *mood*, we are struck by the duality, sometimes even the threefold character, of their meaning. In the midst of an ordinary drama here and there allegory shows through. This allegory does not exhaust all the depth of the drama. The background, on which the dramatic and the allegorical action develops, is the "temper" of these dramas, that is to say their musicality, imagelessness, their unfathomable quality. Here and there we perceive creative attempts to combine the temporal and the non-temporal, to show in mundane action the extra-mundanity of its meaning. These attempts at combination arise from the striving of drama to be suffused with the spirit of music. This conjoint presence of both dramatic and musical quality leads inevitably to symbolism.

D. S. Merezhkovsky defines the symbol as the combination of the disparate in a single thing. In the future, in the opinion of Solov'yov, Merezhkovsky and others, we are due to return to a religious understanding of reality. Does not the musical character of contemporary plays, their *symbolism*, indicate the tendency of drama to become mystery? It is from mystery that drama emerged. It is to mystery that drama is destined to return. Once drama approaches mystery, returns to it, it will inevitably descend from the boards of the stage and extend into life. Do we not have a sign here that life will be transformed into mystery?

Is not a universal mystery about to be played out in life?

Opera, and Wagner's in particular, is also drama. In this drama the musical character emerges into the forefront, but in its proper sense, not a secondary one.

In Wagner, we have the first musician who consciously reached out his hand to tragedy as though in an attempt to facilitate its evolution in the direction of music.

After Wagner, who was still a musician, appear the dramas of Ibsen, who is still a poet, but one who strives towards music. Wagner is a musician who descended to poetry, Ibsen a poet who ascended to music. Both of them have to a substantial extent thrown a bridge across from poetry to music.

Every musical work consists of a series of vibrations of sounds; the perception by the ear of these vibrations as notes is determined by the simplicity of their relations. Not any relation of vibrations is permissible in music. It is essential to select, amongst the limitlessly varied relations, only very simple ones. The expressiveness of melodies, which consists in the selection of these relations, appears to us in other arts either idealization, or typicality, stylization, or schematization.

In A. Böcklin's *The Island of the Dead* we are struck by the correspondence between the figure enclosed in white garments, the rocks the cypress trees and the dark sky (in another version — the twilight background).

This selection only of particular objects expresses the striving to express something uniform. Other colours or tones would have aroused in us a feeling of dissatisfaction; that dissatisfaction would coincide with the dissatisfaction aroused by an unfounded transition into another tone. This sensitivity to dissonances of all kinds has been constantly increasing in recent times. Here we are transferring to other arts something which is peculiar to music. This transference similarly depends upon the greater and greater extension of music, and also on its influence upon the other arts.

In the 19th century music developed swiftly and powerfully. Now it draws our attention willy-nilly. It exercises influence.

An involuntary thought arises about the further character of that influence. Will not all forms of art seek more and more to occupy the position of overtones in relation to the basic tone, i.e. to music?

But the future is unknown . . . .

# NOTES TO "THE FORMS OF ART"

1. Herman von Helmholtz (1821-1894) made fundamental contributions to several branches of science, including physiology, optics, electrodynamics, mathematics and meteorology, and is best known for formulating the law of the conservation of energy. His work *On the Sensation of Tone as a Physiological Basis for the Theory of Music (Die Lehre von den Tonempfindungen)*, in which he combined physiological research with mathematical and physical analysis of wave motion, was published in 1863.

2. Eduard von Hartmann (1842-1906) is best known for his *Philosophy of the Unconscious (Philosophie des Unbewussten)* from 1869. He is regarded as a follower of Schopenhauer.

3. Two lines from Pushkin's sonnet "To the Poet", from 1830.

4. Herbert Spencer (1820-1903) maintained a theory of evolution before Darwin, on the basis of a notion of the inheritance of acquired characteristics. Later he accepted Darwin's idea of natural selection and coined the phrase "the survival of the fittest". He applied biological concepts to the development of human societies, and believed progress to be not accidental, but a necessity. Bely wrote an obituary of him (*Vesy*, 1904 No. 1).

5. Matvey Mikhaylovich Troitsky (1835-1899), an empirical philosopher, published his doctoral dissertation *German Psychology in the Present Century* in 1867. The internal reference is to Dugald Stewart (1753-1828), a Scottish "common sense" philosopher, who from 1785 to 1820 held the chair of moral philosophy at Edinburgh.

6. Mikhail Alexandrovich Vrubel' (1856-1910). showed in his painting features both of Symbolism and of 'style moderne'. He made use of mythological and folklore themes, and is perhaps best known for his depictions of the "Demon", from Lermontov's poem of that name.

7. Axel Gallen (1865-1931), better known after 1905 by the name Gallen-Kallela, was a Finnish modernist painter whose work created something of a furore in the Finnish pavilion at the World Exhibition in Paris in 1900.

8. Vasily Vasil'evich Vereshchagin (1842-1904), is best known for his realistic pictures of battle scenes, largely painted from sketches made on the spot. He also painted "ethnographical" pictures, scenes of daily life in exotic places. He was killed at Port Arthur in the Russo-Japanese War.

9. Eduard Hanslick (1825-1904), a musicologist, was professor at the University of Vienna from 1861 to 1895. His reputation was established by his work *On the Beautiful in Music (Vom Musikalisch-Schönen)* of 1854.

10. Despite Biely's attribution, this quotation is not to be found in the Book of Revelation.

11. The first of these quotations is from Solov'yov's poem "To a friend from Youth", the second from his poem "Les Revenants". Owing to his habit of quoting from memory Bely quite seriously misquoted both. His mistakes have been corrected in translation. See *Stikhotvoreniya Vladimira Solov'yova,*, izd. 3'ye, dopolnennoye, SPb. 1900, pp. 145, 180.

12. Emanual Geibel (1815-1884), German poet and professor of aesthetics at the University of Munich.